The Authorized Biography

by Barry, Robin and Maurice Gibb
as told to David Leaf·

PINNACLE BOOKS ● LOS ANGELES
Published in association with
Delilah Communications, Ltd.

INTRODUCTION

Magic. There is no other word that better describes the Bee Gees. This talented trio of brothers' special blend of magic comes from making music for over twenty years. All along, they've thrilled the world with their sounds.

It has been said that music provides the soundtrack to our lives with the most important moments fixed in our minds by the songs playing at that time. Not only has the Bee Gees music become the soundtrack music of our times, but it's also created an entire musical style based on optimism and hope. The feelings in their music are an affirmation of the promise of the 1960s, the decade that saw the Bee Gees first burst upon the world as international stars. As the passive 1970s finally come to an end, the Bee Gees provide a link with the '60s that will help us all Stay Alive into the uncertain '80s.

The story of the Bee Gees is more than an account of hit records and superstardom. This is a family chronicle filled with the love and triumphs, the problems and setbacks and comebacks that have filled their lives as well as their incredible career. It is almost a modern day fairy tale, with the family not only surviving but prevailing in the end.

The Brothers began singing and making music before they were ten years old. They dreamed of one day being "stars." By the time they were in their late teens, they were internationally known and millionaires as well. The late 1960s were filled with success after success, and they created a body of work that is on a par with all the great songwriters of our time. The songs they've written have been among the most re-corded tunes of the past ten years.

Their initial world-wide breakthrough that began in 1967 wasn't kind to the Bee Gees, and they suffered through a temporary break-up and a relatively quiet period before re-emerging in 1975 as one of the premiere pop groups of the '70s. With their recording for the soundtrack album "Saturday Night Fever," the Bee Gees became the musical phenomenon of the decade.

The record-breaking statistics of that album are only a small part of the Bee Gees story. Everybody, it seems, is a Bee Gees fan. Their music has helped bridge the usually fragmented listening public, so that their audience includes people of all ages and colors, long-time followers and recent converts, record collectors and people who have never bought records before. It is an amazing accomplishment.

The path that the Brothers Gibb have travelled to the pinnacle is a story filled with family love. The Brothers' love for one another and for all members of the Gibb family may seem like a corny concept, but this is an old-fashioned family that believes in traditional ideas. As artists, the Bee Gees are among the most contemporary people making records, but in their private lives, all that matters is their family. Their longevity and popularity isn't a fluke. The emotions the Bee Gees express in their music comes from real feelings and that is a message that nobody misses.

The success of their music is a testament to those ideals, and a lot of hard work. Long ago, the Bee Gees began their career as children singing to adults, and now they are adults singing to all of the "Children of the World."   D.L.

1

CHILDREN

Nervously, they barged on stage, three brothers trailed by two friends. It was a cold December afternoon in 1956, and the five youngsters were about to enter the spotlight of the Gaumont Theatre in Manchester, England.

Barry, at ten the oldest of the group, carried a real guitar, while his twin younger brothers Robin and Maurice carried home-made instruments that couldn't produce a note. That really didn't matter, though, because they weren't there to make music, only to mime to records as was the custom at Saturday matinees all over Manchester. Lots of kids from the audience scrambled for the opportunity to "sing" the hits of the days, and the Gibb brothers were certainly no exception. So there they were, ready to mime to one of older sister Leslie's favorite records. Fortuitous disaster, however, was about to strike.

The man running the Gaumont sound system dropped the record, and as it shattered, so did the Gibbs' hopes of going onstage. The stage fright that had caused hesitation before the record broke could have become panic. But it didn't. After a quick conference, the brothers and friends decided that they would perform without the record. The stage manager set up a microphone, and with Barry strumming his primitive chords and the twins singing in perfect and natural three-part harmony, the Bee Gees were born. Actually, the story began a few years before that.

Hugh Gibb Jr. was a strong-willed young man, more interested in following his own dreams then living out other people's visions of what he should be doing. So with drumsticks in hand, he set out to make a name for himself as a drummer. By 1940, Hugh had found success as a bandleader as well as a drummer. Working on England's Mecca ballroom circuit, Hughie Gibb and his band were a familiar and popular fixture in the north of England as well as in Scotland.

In 1941, Hugh's band was playing in a Manchester ballroom, and as he recalls, he "spotted Barbara Pass in the ballroom dancing. So I got the other fellow on drums, went down and had a dance, took her home." Hugh and Barbara courted for three years before they got married on May 27th, 1944. Very quickly, the Gibbs became three with the birth of a daughter, Leslie, who was born in 1945 in Manchester. Shortly after that, the Gibbs began a long history of travel when they moved to Scotland where Hugh's band played regularly at the Edinburgh Palais. After the end of World War II, Hugh was offered a contract to bring his band to a hotel on the Isle of Man, a holiday island in the Irish Sea between England and Ireland. The Gibbs moved to Douglas, Isle of Man, where the Bee Gees saga really begins.

Barry was the first arrival, September 1, 1946, and being the first born son, he received a bonus on his name. Barry's legal last name is Crompton-Gibb, Sir Isaac Crompton being a famous ancestor of the Gibb's. According to Hugh, Sir Isaac is credited with inventing the mule spinner which revolutionized the cotton industry in England in the 19th century.

A girl and a boy for the Gibbs, Barbara describes her growing family. "Leslie was the eldest and she was a girl. So, of course, the grandparents made a big fuss over her. Then Barry came along, and being a boy, he was made more of a fuss over. When the twins were born, they went berserk." The non-identical twins, Robin and Maurice (pronounced Morris), were born

4

in the early morning hours of December 22, 1949, Robin being the elder by a half-hour. The arrival of two more Gibbs at the same time wasn't a total surprise. The doctor had told Barbara "about four weeks before they were born that I was going to have twins because there were two heartbeats. I had a feeling it was going to be two 'cause I couldn't put my feet on the floor. I couldn't walk."

According to Barbara, the four children were a versatile lot for doting relatives. "They had this little girl [Leslie] who could talk to them like a little lady, the baby twins, and poor old Barry was in the middle of this. I think he got a little bit introverted at the beginning. He used to walk behind me; I'd turn around quickly and he'd fall over me. And he'd be standing there crying. Never made a noise. Tears would roll down his face, but he'd never cry out loud. That was only for a period, and then he came out of that. He was boss of the twins and Leslie was the boss of the lot."

Barry's early quiet nature was also the result of a near fatal childhood accident that scarred him for life. Barbara remembers. "He was about a year and a half old when he poured a boiling pot of tea all over himself. He was seriously ill for about three months, and he didn't talk until he was nearly three because of this. It upset him rather badly. I think this is one of the reasons he used to be quiet because he didn't learn to speak until quite late."

The Bee Gees entire career has been spurred on by a remarkable and dogged determination. Barry thinks that the incident with the scalding teapot may have been his source of resolve. "When you're really injured as a tiny baby, it does something to the rest of your life. Although I don't remember it, I must have gone through extreme agony at some point. That might have made me a fighter or more determined to survive or to make it. It might sound corny as hell, but it is the only thing I can attribute my optimism to. With respect, I don't know anyone else in my family with as much drive as I've got. I've got to prove something all the time, and I don't know why."

Before the twins were born, Barry had another experience that is not only his first conscious memory, but also a startling prescient moment. "On the Isle of Man, when I was about three years old, I was standing on the unloading docks behind an ice cream factory near where we lived in Spring Valley. My first real vision is looking out of a pram. And immediately following that, we were standing on the back of the dock and it was a stage. I remember doing that quite clearly. I don't know if I was singing, but me and a couple of other kids definitely were on a stage."

For both Maurice and Robin, their first memories are unpleasant and identical. The twins each recall being stung by a bee. Maurice's bee sting, though, had a comic conclusion, which was certainly appropriate because he has become a talented comedian. Maurice recalls that after being stung, "I was running down the road. I slipped and fell in water and got the back of my pants soaking wet. I walked all the way home backwards. I didn't want to show anyone my wet bottom." Robin's first pleasant childhood recollection is "eating ice cream on Blackpool Beach in Lancashire when I was five."

Although the twins were similar looking as children, Maurice feels "it's never really like being twins. We are two different people altogether. The only thing in common is our humor and our musical taste. The only time I remember once feeling more like a twin was when Robin was on Barry's bicycle. The brakes weren't working at all, and he hit a car, got bruised all over, and was taken to the hospital. I didn't know about the accident, and I was bruised all over, and I couldn't understand why. Robin had the accident, and I got the bruises too, in exactly the same places. That was the only weird thing. I felt very strange. I just walked around with my backside aching." To Robin, being twins didn't mean anything special nor did it have any advantage, but his only real complaint is that "being born near Christmas, all our presents and everything were given around Christmas." That is a universal lament shared by all of December's children.

Growing up on the Isle of Man and later in Manchester, the early years of the Gibb brothers were filled with some typical and some not so typical mischief. At first, Barry had friends his own age and didn't band together with the twins. But, as Barry remembers, "Mauriee and Robin always tagged along with my mates. Younger brothers always want to be with the oldest, and after a while, the age difference didn't matter. From childhood, we did everything together. The age gap closed as we got older." Barbara recalls how tight-knit the brothers have always been. "They never really made close friends with anybody outside the family. They've always been sufficient to one another." Their constant companionship from a very early age created an unspoken communication among the brothers that is often quite amazing. Barbara explains that "even as small kids, they knew what one another was going to say. They've got this thing between them. It's weird. Without being in the same room, they could all start singing the same song in perfect harmony."

The Brothers Gibb hadn't begun to set the world on fire with their harmony singing yet. In fact, they were doing quite a good job with fire alone. According to Barbara, "Robin was a firebug. He would light fires anywhere, under the bed or in the hedgerow outside the garden. When he was only six, he'd sneak in from school. I'd hear him come through the back door, and then he'd disappear. What he was doing was that he was taking matches out of the kitchen and dashing out again. I used to run around to the front to catch him, but he wouldn't have anything on him. One day, I found a grid, where all the water goes down the drain, full of matches. When he'd hear me coming, he used to stuff them . . . or his father's tools, anything he could sneak out. Goodness, he was terrible." But not alone. As Barbara notes, "Barry was the big man on the escapades. It was always blamed on poor old Robin. They were a backwards fire brigade."

In their youth, the twins could always find some way to cause trouble, but still remain cute. One time, Barbara remembers, "Hugh left some money to pay the electrical bill, about £12 in pound notes, on the mantel shelf over the fireplace. After the children had gone off to school, I got ready to go to pay the bill. When I looked, the money was gone. All I could think of was the twins. The school was only on the corner across the road; I flew across the road. It was playtime, and they were all out in the garden. So I called Maurice over and said, 'Did you see some money on the mantel piece this morning?' 'No,' he said, his eyes huge. 'No. Not me. But Robin's got some paper he found on the mantelpiece. He put it in his windjammer, but it's gone now. He's given it to everybody. Everybody got some.' It was all over the playground. They always used to look at me so innocently, great big eyes."

Maurice recalls that in those days, he "was the goody-goody really. I never got into any bother. Once, I stole a bottle of orange juice at the store, but I got caught. It was the first and last time I ever nicked anything." As in any family, memories often contradict one another and Barbara tells of an incident when Maurice along with Robin "borrowed" more than a bottle of orange juice. "Hugh and I had had a row in the morning. The garbageman had given his wife a bunch of flowers for their anniversary, and I said to

Hugh, 'You've never even bought me a bunch of flowers since we've been married. I never get flowers from anybody!' My mother used to come up to the house every afternoon for a cup of tea with me. We used to sit in the window watching the traffic go by. On the other side of the road was a cemetery. So we're sitting in the window [the afternoon of the fight with Hugh about the flowers] and my mother says, "Whatever is this coming down the road?' All you could see were four little legs. And it was the twins. They were coming down the road with a big wreath they'd pinched off a grave. It said, 'Rest in Peace.' They came in and said, 'Here you are Mummy. Now then, you've got your flowers.' They were so pleased with themselves.

"Robin used to call Maurice 'Woggie," and Maurice used to call Robin 'Bodding.' It was always, 'It's not me, it's Woggie.' And if you mentioned anyone to them, they used to say, 'Oh yes, it's a friend of him.' If it was to do with the twins, anybody they knew was a friend of him!' Unconsciously, Robin could devise words. I'd say, 'Where's such and such a thing?' He'd say, 'It's disagone.' Barry was always quieter. He'd sing at the drop of a hat for anybody. But normally, he was quiet. Maurice was always going to be a painter and a decorator. He used to keep paper money-bits of paper he'd make himself, and he'd keep them in his 'office.' He was always giving people a job. And he really believed this. He put you on the payroll for £20 a week."

As children, the brothers' personalities were only beginning to take shape. There was no love of music yet, but the origins of the Bee Gees were there. For instance, Robin has always been considered the most highly imaginative of the brothers, particularly when it comes to storytelling. Robin's lyrics and plaintive vibrato singing were the trademarks of the early Bee Gees hits, and it was Robin who showed the first interest in writing. His favorite stories were those of "Nod-

9

die and Biggie" and the first book he ever read, **The Little Engine That Could** may have been self-inspiring. Slight of build and tremulous of voice (when singing), Robin's onstage image was once one of extreme fragility. Like the **Little Engine . . .**, Robin possesses a persistence and determination that goes beyond a surface impression of insecurity. Robin remembers the days when he "used to sort of compose stories in school, pretty serious writing with a sense of humor. I hated school, so when they used to do sums and everything, I used to write things. They used to belt me for it, but I still used to do it."

Although the Bee Gees are noted for their lyrical and composing skills, they spent very little time in school, and they pride themselves on being self-educated. Robin recalls that "Maurice and I sang in the school choir at Christmas carol concerts, and when it came to 'God Save The Queen,' we'd sing together and throw the whole choir." For the most part, though, Robin explains that the brothers "had a very scattered school-life, not much of a school-life at all. I hated school, and I still do." Robin's unfond feelings towards his schooling were present from the very beginning. Barbara describes a typical school day. "The first thing in the morning, Robin wouldn't get up until the fire was lit and roaring up the chimney. Then he'd stand there shivering. I'd get them off to school. Then, there'd be a little knock on the door, and Robin would be back. He was cold or his nose was blocked up and he couldn't breathe. These were only little things, because I used to take him back to school and he was quite happy. He would never leave me; Robin always wanted to be at home with me. The other two couldn't have cared less whether I was there or not. They've always been like that. Robin was always a little bit dependent, right up to about fourteen, 'cause he was such a gentle little soul. He was mischievous and did all the damage, but you wouldn't have thought so."

Robin confirms this. "I was a little swine actually. I didn't know it at the time, but I look back now and I know I was. For the things I did, they put kids in reform school. Same as Barry as well. We used to go and set fire to golf courses and things like that. We never did anything that could have harmed people. But we did a lot of damage to open land. We were very young and came from the kind of area where we weren't the only kids like that . . . my best friend, who lived down the road from us in Northern Grove in Manchester in '57, went with us. We used to go into houses that had been vacated and do a lot of wrecking. He was found the following day walking down the road and was picked up and sent to reform school because he'd had a previous record. Me and Barry went to court and we were put on probation."

The Gibb family had spent a lot of time shuttling between the Isle of Man and England, and they finally moved back to Manchester "for good" in 1955. Hugh remembers that Barbara "felt she'd like to go back to the mainland again" to be near her family on a regular basis. The youngest Gibb brother, Andy, was born in Manchester before the family moved to Australia. It was in Manchester, though, that the musical career of the Gibb brothers began. Rock 'n' roll was in its infancy in '55, and the Gibb kids were swept up in the excitement although it was older sister Leslie who was the really big fan. A typical young girl in the mid-1950's, she loved Elvis the most as well as the Everly Brothers and English favorites Tommy Steele and Cliff Richards. Bill Haley and the Comets were the first big group and had an enormous influence on the Gibb brothers as far as creating an interest in performing. Barry describes how "we used to make guitars from cheese boxes. We'd take the round piece from the bottom and the planks from the side as the neck. We'd use Dad's fuse wire, for strings. It made no sound, but we became Bill Haley and the Comets."

The erstwhile Comets were then residing on Keppel Road in the Manchester suburb of Chorlton-cum-Hardy. The local cinema on the corner, a branch of the Gaumont chain, was the Saturday hangout for the neighborhood kids where they'd thrill to the serialized adventures of Dan Dare or Flash Gordon before the feature which might be a Zorro film. Before the films started, there was often an extra attraction, and Robin recalls the moment that catalyzed the brothers into becoming public performers. "We were sitting in the Gaumont one December morning and this kid came on stage miming to an Elvis record with a toy guitar." According to Robin, "he was only a little kid, but he was doing it well. And we thought, 'Why don't we do that?' " Kids miming to records was a regular feature of the Saturday Gaumont program, so the theatre manager wasn't surprised when the Gibb brothers approached him and asked if they could mime to a record the next Saturday. As Maurice recalls, "We had phony guitars that dad bought us; Barry had the only real one." The brothers, along with friends Paul Frost and Kenny Oricks "rehearsed" all week. They nicknamed themselves "The Rattlesnakes," and armed with one of Leslie's 78 rpm records, they set out for the Gaumont. According to the legend, the sound man at the Gaumont dropped and broke the record they were to mime to, forcing the brothers into a momentous decision, momentous considering what has come since. Robin: "I think it was my suggestion that we go on and actually sing. Maurice said, 'You're out of your box.' Barry said, 'You know we can't go on ourselves.' I said, 'Let's go on and sing; we've been doing it every day!"

As Barry recalls, the week before their performance was the first time the brothers had sung together.

"During that week, for some reason, we started to actually sing. We discovered that we had voices . . . three little kids, and we were able to harmonize with each other. We started to sing in harmony from the very beginning. It staggered me more than anybody, and I was only a kid." That one week of singing hadn't exactly over-prepared the Gibbs for their singing debut. The fact that their only instrument was Barry's guitar didn't serve to increase their confidence, so it took a lot of convincing and courage before they decided to sing.

Barry explains that after the week of practicing and looking forward to doing it, "the momentum was too much for us. We couldn't not go onstage. We just had to do it. Our opportunity was there." Maurice picks up the story. "The manager put a microphone in front of us and we sang, 'As I walk by the seaside . . . I Love You Baby' by Paul Anka. Or maybe it was 'Wedding Bells' by Tommy Steele." Nobody really remembers for sure what song it was, but Maurice does recall that the promised sixpence wasn't forthcoming. Not that it mattered. "We never got paid. We used to do it for the fun of it. The fun and the screaming." Robin: "All the kids went 'Yeah!' We were sort of an instant hit. But we wanted to do bigger things now. The manager of the Gaumont gave us a couple of bob, couple of shillings, about twenty-five cents, to go down the road to the Odeon and do the same thing. And we thought, 'Great!' and we caught the number 18 bus." Although the bus fare equalled their "artist's fee," the Gibb brothers had become famous, as Robin recalls. "We opened a local suburban paper the following day, and there we were, a picture of us singing at the Odeon. The first picture of the Bee Gees ever taken."

According to Barry, after the Gaumont and Odeon debuts, "our whole theme in life was to be discovered. We would stand on street corners and sing. It was the

13

feeling of standing in front of an audience that was so amazing. We'd never seen anything like it. We were very young, but it made an enormous impression. We didn't want to do anything else but make music. That put a dent in our education to a great extent."

The Gibb brothers, now named "Wee Johnny Hays and The Bluecats," loved to mime to records and sing in theatres. Even though this was show business at the most amateur level, performing of any kind was all-important to them. When they weren't singing in public, Maurice remembers, "we used to pretend to have a TV station underneath the house. We'd get a big old cardboard box, and take broken binocular parts, put it in one end of the box, cut a square hole on the other end and look through it like a TV camera. Barry used to be the newsman, and we'd 'film' it with the box. That was the kind of games we used to play as kids."

It was in the winter of 1957, following their first miming efforts, that the brothers began to make music in earnest. Barry: "I first became conscious of music when I was nine. On my birthday in '55, I got a trumpet. But the second day I had it, Leslie broke it during an argument." Hugh had watched his oldest son making banjo-like "stringed-instruments" and recalls how Barry "used to strum along on this pre-historic thing. I knew a guy who had a music store in Manchester, and I went to see if he'd got any second-hand guitars. For £4, I got a beautiful guitar and leather case that was Barry's Christmas present. He used to sit around the garden wall, singing to the kids in the street." That gift was a surprise for Barry "because I didn't think I was going to get it. A guy who lived across the road from us had just come out of the Army, and he'd been stationed in Hawaii. He couldn't play the guitar, but he could play Hawaiian chords. And he tuned the guitar for me and showed me what Hawaiian chords were. And I'm still playing those

14

chords now with a few extensions of what he taught me. I never learned the guitar." As Robin notes, "We've never been taught music. We can't even read music now. I could go and learn it tomorrow, but there's no reason. We even do our own string arrangements."

Back in 1957, the brothers weren't using any strings other than those on Barry's guitar. Barbara recounts how the family first found out about the boys' developing musical talent. "Hugh's father had a bad stroke, and we used to bring him over every Saturday afternoon to watch the cricket matches on television. I used to go out shopping, and I'd come in, and he'd still be there watching the television." Hearing music emanating from the brother's bedroom, Barbara asked Hugh Sr. if "the kids are bothering you?' He said, 'No. No. They're just singing.' I said, 'No. They've got the gramophone on.' He said, 'No. It's the boys singing.' I thought, 'He doesn't know what he's talking about.' So I went into their room and there's the three of them, two little tots on the bed and Barry. And they're singing, 'Lollipop!' It was fantastic, and I couldn't believe it. And they just looked at me. And he [Hugh Sr.] said, 'Oh. They've been singing like that for weeks.' He'd been coming over and listening to this every Saturday afternoon. It just hadn't dawned on me. And then of course, when Hugh came home, we had them sing it for him and they were thrilled."

In addition to "Lollipop," Everly Brothers' songs like "Wake Up Little Susie" were special favorites of the Gibb brothers. Maurice explains that 'we'd just add a third part to their two-part harmony." That musical harmony was the sweetest part of the Gibbs' family life at that point. The return to Manchester from the Isle of Man wasn't a happy one. As Hugh recalls, "After living on a holiday island, Manchester seemed so gloomy and depressive. Barbara's sister Audrey was toying with the idea of going to Australia so I said to Barbara, 'What do you think? It might be good for the boys.' ' Barry explains that the move "had a lot to do with our escapades as children. We did get into a lot of trouble. We broke the law about as much as you can. We had a policeman go off a cliff into the river chasing us on his bicycle. He was only slightly injured. We lit a lot of fires, burnt a lot of places down . . . all empty except for the time Robin burnt down somebody's shop." Robin half-seriously relates the time that "a very friendly policeman came and said to my dad: 'Look, if you wanna avoid your kids going to reform school, emigrate to Australia.' "

Barry and Robin's forays into juvenile delinquency were only a small part of the reason for the move. As Barry notes, "Our father was really having trouble making ends meet in England. Also, the climate was terrible, I remember our parent's looking at travel brochures and getting very excited. They wanted a new life." To Barry, the move wasn't upsetting. "I didn't care where I lived. I remember as a kid that it was dark and bleak. To me, looking at the travel pamphlets [and the trip] and seeing half the world on the way there was the greatest adventure of my life. I was twelve years old. You look forward to things like that; you don't really think about where you're leaving."

Before the Gibb family left England, the brothers gave a real singing performance that Barry characterizes as "the first time we ever had a rapport between us and an audience. It wasn't kids who came to the cinema." Hugh Gibb epxlains: "I was playing the Russel St. Club, which was licensed premises, kids weren't allowed in. One night, the owner, Ernie Darbisher, who was a friend of mine, smuggled the boys in the back door. I was on the drums, and they went onstage in little short pants and sang 'All I Have To Do Is Dream' and 'Lollipop' and one other and brought the place down." Barbara notes that "we were on the verge of emigrating, and it was really a farewell week we had at the club." The boys' performance, Hugh recalls, was rewarded with a gift of "half a crown, two shillings which is the equivalent to about fifty cents now. And my brother smuggled them out the back door and took them home."

The performance? Barry remembers that "the audience thoroughly enjoyed what we did, and they applauded and they stood up. And it knocked us sideways. Now we know it was because we were kids because we weren't all that good." Barbara points out "that it was just cute. It was good, because you don't find kids that can sing like they can in harmony, but it was cute. I didn't think, 'Oh, I'm going to have big stars.' Not at that point." To the brothers, that show was acceptance. Barry felt that "we were on our way. When you think of where we were, we weren't on our way anywhere." Except Australia.

The Gibb family had moved around quite a bit, but always within shouting distance of England. Australia is over twelve thousand miles from the Gibbs' homeland, so it was an adventurous step for them to leave and head for a distant and somewhat alien land. Remarkably, there was little sentiment involved in the move, no sense of a nostalgic longing that they might feel for England once they left. It was without a backwards glance that they bade farewell to their home and headed towards what they hoped would be a new and better life.

The ship ride to Australia included some Gibb brothers' extracurricular activities that were typical of their rapidly developing show business ambitions. Never ones to miss an opportunity to perform, they constantly sang to their captive audience, this time going by the name of Barry and the Twins. Barbara recalls that "on the boat, we had to have all the children

17

off the decks and in bed by 9:00. I used to put them to bed, and we'd go up to this nightclub afterwards. And we'd come out at 12:00 and see them in pajamas . . . at the end of the top deck with a crowd of people around them. And they were singing. All the way over."

"he seemed really interested and went and spoke to somebody. He came back and said, 'Yeah, all right. It can be done.' " There was an amplification system and the track management thought that the singing might prove to be a little bit of entertainment between the races. The track got quite a bargain, because they told the Gibbs, "You're only kids and you're too young to receive payment for such a things. But if people throw money on the track, that's fine." As Barry notes, "we weren't really interested in the bread anyway; we just wanted to do it. We did three songs, our own songs, which were 'Let Me Love You,' 'Twenty Miles to Blueland' and one other. We picked up about £3/10 off the track out of the sawdust."

The brothers' debut in Australia was quite auspicious, and they became regulars at the track. During one of their earliest performances, a racing driver named Bill Goode heard a lot of commotion from the crowd and left the racing pits to find out what was happening. He heard the kids singing, and was impressed enough to find out where they lived and let them know he wanted to talk to their parents. None of the Gibbs remembers the exact time of Bill Goode's discovery. Barbara recalls that "it was weeks before I found out what they were doing. I thought they were just going to watch the races. Until one night they came home with the pockets of their jeans stuffed with pennies. They couldn't walk. And they were complaining, 'Nobody's discovered us yet.' " So it was probably late in 1959 that Bill Goode noticed the brothers singing. Barbara remembers the "night after Bill Goode had heard them. They never met Goode, but one of the boys who worked in the pits came over to them and said, 'Tell your mum to ring this number. It's to do with recording.' So Barry says, 'How much money will we get?' " And the man told the brothers £2,000. Actually, the man told them they might earn as much as

21

£2,000, but when the kids got home they said, "Mommy, you ring this number in the morning and we're going to get £2,000."

When Mrs. Gibb called the next day, she found out that a number of people were interested in helping the boys' career along. Bill Goode had a friend, Bill Gates, who was a DJ in Brisbane. Goode brought Gates to the Gibb's home to hear the boys sing. Hugh was still out working in the bush country, and Barbara didn't want to be the only adult representing her sons. So Barbara's cousin came over from his nearby home to be there when the important visitors arrived. As Barbara remembers, "they came and listened to the boys, and they were absolutely knocked out." Bill Gates points out that "the raw talent of the Bee Gees was apparent. The harmonies were fantastic. Barry was able to write a new song in five minutes."

Meanwhile, out in the bush country, Hugh was getting telegrams saying, 'You better get home." By the time he returned to Brisbane, his sons were about to make their first recordings. Hugh recalls that "Bill Gates had a big radio program every lunch hour called 'Midday Platter Chatter.' He got the boys in the studio on a Sunday and recorded them on tape. And every day, he'd play one of the tapes." Hugh Gibb, who is very much a total show business personality, also tends to romanticize his memories of his sons' career. So it is not a surprise that his tales often directly contradict those of his sons. According to Barry, "Gates' show on Brisbane's 4BH was a half hour. We would tune in, and he might play one of our tapes." Whatever actually happened, everybody agrees with Barry's statement that the airplay "did us an enormous amount of good." The Gibb Brothers were beginning to make a name for themselves, and that name was B.G.'s. Bill Gates had taken note of all the B.G. initials (Bill Goode, Barry Gibb and himself) and christened the group. So the

Gibbs became the B.G.'s. A few years later, it was elongated to Bee Gees where it has come to stand for the Brothers Gibb.

That name might have been impossible if the brothers' older sister Leslie hadn't been shy. As she recalls, "When the boys were first starting, Bill Gates wanted me to sing with them. I was fourteen at the time, and every time Bill Gates came 'round to the house, I used to lock myself in my bedroom to avoid being brought into the group. I was scared stiff of the idea." With the recent rise of baby brother Andy to pop stardom, Leslie is the only Gibb sibling who isn't a singing millionaire.

At that point in the group's "career," Bill Gates bowed out, explaining that he was just a DJ and not a businessman, and there wasn't anything more he could do for them. So Hugh took over, and when he wasn't working his regular job, he was doing all he could to further the B.G.'s. Hugh remembers that the group's next break came when television started up in Brisbane around 1960. "We auditioned for one of the variety shows, 'Anything Goes,' on the non-commercial network, ABC (the Australian equivalent of the BBC). Right away, they signed us." Hugh recounts how "to get a vocal balance, they had a boom mike, and the twins stood on boxes on either side of Barry to bring them up to the same height."

The next stop was at the commercial networks, where the Bee Gees auditioned for a monthly show on Channel 9 called "Brisbane Tonight." The open audition had attracted a studio full of kids and ambitious parents, and it was past ten o'clock before the Bee Gees had a chance to show their stuff. Hugh describes how he "cued the boys and said, 'Look. When you go in, don't mind all these people here. Work to this table where these two men are.' Wilbur Kemtwell was at the table; he was the musical director. It was a typical audition. The boys went up with the guitar, and they sang one of their own compositions while the two men were talking among themselves. After they sang, all the people in the studio just cheered. Wilbur took his glasses off and asked, 'Can you do another one?' They sang all night for him."

The Bee Gee's TV appearances produced a lot of interest in Brisbane TV circles, and they were so popular that they became regulars on a Channel 7 program called "Cottee's Happy Hour" which was sponsored by Cottee, a soft drink and jam manufacturer. Because the boys were so young, they had to get permission from the headmaster at school to appear on the show every week. On each show, the group would perform three or four songs within their own segment, but it was never the Bee Gees' own program.

The brothers were already hard working pros by the end of 1960, but they were still young and fun loving. That often caused a bit of a commotion, especially at the TV stations. Barbara: "They were naughty. Because Hugh had the job at the time, I used to take them to the television studio alone. Before they went on to do the show, we used to sit in a little foyer. But they wouldn't sit. They used to disappear. At one point, they climbed up the television mast. When all the executives arrived, they'd say, 'This place is lousy with Bee Gees.' "

With all the TV exposure, the group began to be in demand for local "live" shows. Their first personal appearances were on the vaudeville circuit. It is a British custom that during the performance of plays like "Jack and the Beanstalk" or "Cinderella," there is entertainment onstage in between scenes. Maurice recalls that it was at places like the "Rialto Theatre in Brisbane, they had us featured on the billboard, 'Featuring the B.G.'s.' We'd go out and sing while they changed the set. We'd do 'Run Samson Run' or some other Neil Sedaka song, and one other song, and one of our own. We'd try to break our songs across to them. The kiddies loved it. They'd cheer, 'Hey great,' and then they're back to 'Jack and the Beanstalk' again."

The Bee Gees began performing in nightclubs and bars. It was a very strange atmosphere for children. The Gibb brothers usually found themselves appearing exclusively in front of adults. As the engagements got further apart, often as far as one hundred miles from home, Hugh Gibb had to make a decision. "Is it my job or is it going to be them? I felt their future's going to be stronger than mine, so, to be quite frank, they kept us. I gave up my work just to drive them around. They were only kids; they had to have somebody. I never wanted to be their manager, but by force of circumstances I had to be."

A better manager the Bee Gees really couldn't have found. Hugh always had his boys' best interests in mind, and he combined that with his show business experience. Rehearsing them relentlessly, Hugh taught them everything from how to walk on stage, to how to smile and be nice to an audience. And when he could, he'd even sit in on drums to provide the boys with a firm beat. He'd even arrange the program. As Robin recalls, "We had to appeal to adults so my father, who was and is a very big Mills Brothers fan, had us do a lot of Mills Brothers songs on the nightclub circuit." The Bee Gees act at that time included such staples as "Alexander's Ragtime Band," "My Old Man's A Dustman," and "Does Your Chewing Gum Loose Its Flavor." Whenever they could, the Bee Gees would slip in something they really liked. Their favorites and major influences at the time were Ray Charles and Neil Sedaka; later on Roy Orbison and Otis Redding were strong vocal influences. In listening to Robin's moving 1978 hit rendition of the Beatles' "Oh! Darling," one can hear a bluesy feel is a direct descendant of Ray Charles.

Working the hotel/vaudeville circuit, the group developed what Barry termed "a comedy act with harmony. It was a great education to vaudeville because you not only perform your own act, but you do comedy with the resident comedian. Really a great training ground." Maurice explains, "My father knew exactly what those audiences wanted. If we were cute little kids, any bit of comedy would have them laughing their heads off, saying 'they're so cute.' We used to do slapstick. For instance, we'd be singing 'Puff the Magic Dragon' and every time Robin sang 'Puff,' I'd get sprayed in the face. Moms and Dads loved that. We had a lot of comedy routines. I was always the one who got suckered, always the straight man. Robin was the funny one, the cheeky little cute look. Barry was the older brother, looking after us. It was always visual comedy. Sort of like Abbott and Costello."

Musically, the boys were singing songs that would appeal to adults, and Maurice attributes that to the fact that "my father always wanted us to be like another Mills Brothers. We were wearing tuxedos, shoes always polished, Brylcream in our hair." Whether it was their comic rendition of "Puff . . ." or a send-up of "Dear One," the object was always for the brothers to be cute. Away from their shows, it was songwriting that the brothers concentrated on as well as their harmony singing. Maurice remembers that "we never really had any other ambition of being anything except singers. It was fun for us. We loved to make people laugh, loved the sound of the applause, applauding our singing. Barry sang the middle lead vocal, Robin the low part, and I'd do the high harmony."

Robin's memories of those early days aren't as positive as Maurice's. "All I know is I didn't like Australia. I was only a kid, but I never really liked it. I didn't like the work either 'cause of the songs we were singing. I used to complain, but it didn't make any difference. I had to go and do it." Maurice puts another perspective on Robin's feelings. "I wouldn't say he was mad about it, but I know he didn't mind it. I didn't. We were doing something that was new to us. Naturally, we wanted to sing teenager songs, but we were kids and we couldn't attract teenage audiences." So the songs the brothers really wanted to sing, from Sedaka's "Breaking Up Is Hard to Do" to Charles' "What'd I Say" took a back seat to other numbers like "Dinah" and "Bye Bye Blackbird."

Doing even those songs was exciting for the three Gibbs because they had serious show business aspirations at that early age. Maurice recalls that "almost every time we came off stage, the audience was going 'More! More! More!' in the background. We'd go, 'Oh!' and Dad would say 'You killed them tonight.' We'd go out there and do one more song, and they'd love it. Dad would say, 'Always leave them wanting' and he'd usher us out the back door. And the next week, we'd get another booking for that club because 'we left them wanting' as our father would say. Robin used to love it when he'd hear the 'More! More! More!'s."

Barbara remembers that her children loved to perform so much that they couldn't ever relax. "In all the years they'd been working when we lived in Australia, I think they had two weekends when they didn't work. And on those, they used to pester us to ring up all the agencies to see if anybody had got sick and needed somebody to sit in. They just didn't know what to do with themselves." Maurice confirms his mother's recollection. "We just enjoyed doing it. We couldn't wait for the weekends to start singing again. We'd do a show Friday night, one on Saturday afternoon, one Saturday evening, and then a later show on Saturday . . . shows

Sunday afternoon and one in the evening. The rest of the week was off." Throughout the early 1960's, the Bee Gees played weekend gigs in the Queensland area. Sometimes, they'd sing at dingy nightclubs and hotels like the Sandgate, the Bonneville and the Oxley; other times, they might do their show at a regular theatre. For the most part, though, they played to adults. They were making a living, supporting a family of seven, but in their own eyes, they weren't getting anywhere. As Hugh notes, "The boys wanted to go to Sydney, which is like going to New York." They wanted to get to the big time. Their ambitions were very strong. Barry recalls the time he "ran away from home only to return almost immediately. It was inside me. I had to go to Sydney."

One of the regular spots that the group played was the Palm Lounge which was located in Surfer's Paradise, a big holiday resort on the Queenland coast in Australia. The Bee Gees often went there for the weekend to play at the various hotels. After one especially long engagement at the Palm in 1961, Hugh and the boys decided to make the trip to Sydney. Hugh remembers how "we were to leave Barbara in Brisbane, and I'd take the boys. We set off in the car. We didn't know what the devil we were going to do when we got there." The Gibbs had only gotten about a half hour outside of Brisbane when they stopped for gas. It was then that Hugh realized he'd forgotten his wallet, so they went back home. In their brief absence, the owner of the Palm Lounge had called to book the boys for two weeks. They decided they would play the two-week engagement and go to Sydney from there. They stayed in Surfer's Paradise for eighteen months.

The year and a half in Surfer's Paradise was a holding period for the Bee Gees. There wasn't any career progress, but they were honing their craft. Virtually every weekend, they would work at both the Palm

Lounge and at the Beachcomber, and the constant work was turning them into professionals. Even so, they never missed a chance to play a trick. Barbara recounts, "We used to play the Southport Hotel which was in the same area as the Beachcomber. They would really play me up. Just before they went onstage, they'd disappear into the gent's toilet, where I couldn't follow them, to tune up. And I used to be petrified because their singing used to go right through the whole place. Everybody could hear them tuning up and singing. And I couldn't go in and tell them when it was time to go onstage. They knew very well I couldn't go into this place, so that's why they went. But they never missed a cue. They were very professional always."

Barbara recalls another, more violent incident that was a perfect example of the trouper's adage that "the show must go on." "Robin had a crush on one of the little girls in the chorus. He was only about twelve. And he would watch her when he was onstage. We were told by the stage manager that anyone standing in the wings would be fined. Robin insisted on standing in the wings to watch this girl . . . We were sharing a dressing room with the two very top comedians in Australia, men who'd been in the business for years. Barry, of course, is the boss, and he stood at the bottom of the stairs and shouted, 'Robin. Come down here.' Robin wouldn't, and he stood and stood. And Barry was getting madder and madder. So Barry dashed upstairs, got Robin by the scruff of the neck and threw him down into the dressing room. And they're fighting on the floor, in their stage clothes. And these two comedians were watching them with their eyes . . . any minute, the boys' cue music is going to start [Hugh's old theme, 'The World is Waiting for the Sunrise']. It started, and these two comedians are still watching them. They got up. dusted themselves down, and they went onstage, did their act perfectly, dashed

29

down the stairs and immediately started in again. They were really mad. Barry because Robin hadn't done as he had been told the first time. It was frightening. I I had some really bad times with them, but looking back, they were fun times too."

In the early '60's, the Australian pop scene was headed by a singer named Col Joye. "In 1962," Barry recalls, "Col was doing a tour of the provinces and happened to pass through Surfer's Paradise where we were working. We were desperate to get to meet him, and he happened to be rehearsing no more than about one hundred yards from our house, in a hall for his show. We thought, 'This is the next step. If we can meet this guy, we can sell him a song, and we're on our way.' We all talked about it, but nobody would go over and say hello. So I said, 'I'm going. It's the only chance we've got.' It ended up with me walking across the road to this hall with Dad about one hundred yards behind with his date book. We got there and I said to this man that I would like to meet with Col Joye. What I didn't know was that I was speaking to Kevin Jacobsen, Col's brother. When I first said, 'Hi, we want to see Col Joye,' he must have been thinking, 'Who's this? Go away.'" With great confidence Barry said, "We're a singing group, and we write songs." To Barry and everyone's surprise, Kevin replied, "Hang around for a minute; Col is on his way out." Barry describes the arrival of the "pop star" as Col came through "with sunglasses, like Presley. Everybody was a Presley in those days. We said hello and I said, 'I'd like to sing you some of the songs we've written with an interest, a view to you recording them if possible.' So he said, 'Oh sure." I couldn't believe it. He came over to the house, and we sat down and played for him. He wasn't totally knocked out by the material as much as he was mesmerized by the way we were singing and harmonizing at that age. He said, 'You've got to come to Sydney and make a record!' " One song that Col especially liked, "Straight of Love," impressed him enough that he eventually recorded it. According to Barry, "it was the first solid sign we'd ever had that we might be going somewhere."

It was in 1962 that the Bee Gees were brought to Sydney by Col and Kevin, who became their agent. Maurice remembers that trip as a turning point. "We wanted to be well-known. It was nice to be heard on the radio and be recognized and that sort of thing. But we never looked at it as a long-term thing. Neither did my father. We were just doing it as something to do, something we loved doing. When we went to Sydney, meeting the big stars of Australia, particularly Col Joye, then all of a sudden, stardust hit us. 'Wow, it's great to be a star, flash cars and nice houses, swimming pools . . ." We thought, 'This is for us.' I think that's when it first hit us that it'd be great to be successful."

Kevin had arranged for the Bee Gees trip to Sydney so that they could perform at a Chubby Checker concert. Barry remembers that show as "incredible. For that time, it was amazing. Thousands of screaming kids. Not screaming at us, but it was a sight for us to see, to be part of it." Chubby Checker (the King of the Twist) was the American star of the moment and he closed the show. Johnny O'Keefe was the Australian rock star of the moment, and he was on third to last. Somebody decided to put the Bee Gees in between. Barry describes that as "a very frigtening experience. We sang some rock 'n' roll songs, but we weren't a rock 'n' roll group. Then we sang things like 'Alexander's Ragtime Band' . . . enough to get us into deep trouble. We just didn't know what kids wanted. We'd worked in nightclubs. We didn't think anybody was ever going to thrust us on kids. As much as we wanted it, we didn't think it was ever going to happen to us."

While their appearances with Chubby Checker didn't meet with any mass acclaim, it was the first big step in the group's career. "Our first recording contract," Robin points out, "came in 1963 as a result of the Chubby Checker concert in Sydney. Now in Sydney, that's where all the labels are. You don't get signed up anywhere else but Sydney. So Festival Records approached us with a contract and," Robin sardonically recounted, "we recorded our first flop which was a record called 'The Battle of the Blue and Grey'."

Along with the Festival contract came another upheaval in the Gibb family. Having moved from Brisbane to Surfer's Paradise, they again uprooted themselves in early '63 and moved to the Sydney suburb of Lakemba. Even with their newfound status as recording artists, the Bee Gees career wasn't a particularly hot item. They were just playing bigger clubs. It's true they were headliners, but for an Australian act, headlining is the end of the line. It's just an endless string of engagements at nightclubs and returned soldier's clubs and TV variety shows. In one respect, it was the beginning of a new part of the Bee Gees career, but it very quickly became hard work. The Bee Gees' often brutal schedule made it impossible for them to continue in school. Barry had dropped out of school in '61 when he turned fifteen, and Maurice and Robin followed his example in December of '63. Maurice explains that "it sort of came to the crunch when we knew that this is going to be our career. That's why we weren't that interested in school, and why we left. We wanted to stick with our career. That was the time really that it became important. Not being appreciated was an awful thing, and being appreciated was a great thing. Naturally, we knew it was the best, and we went for the best."

As the Bee Gees' career took over their lives, it also had enveloped the entire Gibb family. Hugh managed them and Barbara was in charge of wardrobe. Wherever the Bee Gees career took them, the family followed, lending support. In return, the Bee Gees were the breadwinners. Maurice doesn't "find it embarrassing at all to say we supported our family. We did for many years. Our father put in as many years as we put in. And my mom did just as much, always looking after our clothes and getting us together. We always looked after our family 'cause they looked after us. Leslie must have felt left out, though, because the three boys were our dad's dream."

The brothers' dream of success as recording stars had gotten off to a poor start with the failure of their first and self-penned single, "The Three Kisses of Love" and "The Battle of the Blue and Grey." As Robin notes, "It bombed. It didn't matter to us. We just wanted to see our name on a record. We didn't care if it was a hit or not. It was very hot with one guy at (radio station) 2SM in Sydney, and he was playing it all the time. It didn't do anything. The follow-up [in June of '63] was 'Timber' and that did exactly what the title implied, fell. So we went back into the studio nine months later, and brought out a record called 'Peace of Mind' which did exactly what the previous two did. Then, we started our experimental stage because the Beatles were happening, and we thought we'd get some inspiration from this group, 'they're doing so well overseas.' A British group, we're British living in Australia, surely we can do something. We wrote a song called 'Claustrophobia,' and I won't tell you what happened to that. After the first four or five flop records, we started to get more concerned about the records being hits."

The Bee Gees' disappointment was beginning to grow as they watched one release after another sink in the charts. The arrival of the Beatles on the Australian scene in '64 only served to increase the Bee Gees' sense of defeat. As Maurice recalls, "We could see all the teenagers going mad over these guys. We said, 'Boy, I wish we were like them,' things like that. They were getting screaming kids and being mobbed and all that. We'd never seen anything like that before. But also important was the admiration we had; naturally, we were all influenced by them." Hugh angrily points out that the Australians were blind to their own Bee Gees once the Beatles arrived. "People never realized that the Bee Gees had been recording longer than the Beatles had. But when the Beatles became strong, then the Bee Gees started to be compared with the Beatles, as though they were copying. In fact, they altered their recording style, but it didn't work. The boys were getting pretty uptight. We used to say, 'Don't they realize they've got the Australian Beatles here?' "

While the Gibbs' frustration is understandable, the 1964 Bee Gees weren't in the same league as the Beatles. While the Brothers Gibb certainly had a professional act, their own records and compositions of the time just didn't measure up to what the Beatles were doing. And, of course, the Beatles were much older than the Bee Gees. After all, in 1964, the twins were still only fourteen. They were precocious, yes, but they weren't the Australian Beatles. Considering their age, they already were quite successful and quite good.

The Bee Gees' earliest records were sent out into a vacuum. Being a group of adolescents playing to adults, they weren't a marketable commodity. The key to selling records in those days was to appeal to a teenage audience, and the Bee Gees weren't playing to teenagers. It was primarily a "mums and dads" crowd that came to see their nightclub appearances, and this was not the record buying public. Robin, who is a student of the record charts and probably knows as much about the workings of the record industry as any executive in the business, explains that in Australian days, "I used to examine the charts and the radio set up. That's why I wanted to have hit records. But I had the erratic sort of position of being a kid as well. Kids are very impatient, and though I knew a lot about hits, I never knew where to start. When you're a kid, although you're living for every day, you think time's so short. We were doing nightclubs and things like that. But I've got a very funny impression of the way Australia used to treat the Bee Gees. In retrospect, when I look back and play some of the records, for that period in Australia, they should have been hits. But it was just that nobody would take the time to take the Bee Gees seriously, which is a crime for anyone. To me, it's criminal to ignore a record because of what you might think [of the artist]. Our first record company gave us a cold hard time."

In a slight defense of Festival Records, Barry points out that "Festival was under the same situation we were. We did not appeal to kids because we were kids, and it was hard for the people at Festival to sell us. But Fred Marks [Festival's president] took the wrong view in my estimation. He didn't give us time in the studio to develop. We were allowed two hours on a Saturday afternoon because the big label stars were using the studio all the rest of the time. We weren't selling records so they would say, 'Get it done boys. It won't be a hit anyway'. That was the attitude. I remember that clearly." Hugh recalls, "One time, the boys had twelve minutes to do a vocal because the engineer had to catch his train." Maurice adds, "If we wanted strings on the record, they'd say, 'who the hell do you think you are, Kruschev?' "

Throughout 1963 and 1964, the Bee Gees performing career flourished despite their lackluster recording efforts. There were frequent television appearances on the "Bandstand" program, and in April of '64, they were featured on their own TV special. The producer of that program was Nat Kipner, a man who returns to the story a little later on as one of the Bee Gees' first supporters within the record industry.

The Bee Gees continued to make records. They also continued to have no hits. Having failed with songs of their own composition, the brothers decided to record someone else's tunes. The result was an October '64 release, "Turn Around Look At Me" b/w a TV theme, "The Travels of Jamie McPheeters." In April of '65, they tried again with an imitative version of Steve Alaimo's "Every Day I Have To Cry." The flip side, Barry's "You Wouldn't Know" featured an important first, Robin's debut as a lead vocalist. Between those two disks, the Bee Gees also made a record with Trevor Gordon. Barry wrote the two tunes, "House Without Windows" and "And I'll Be Happy." The disk was released under the name Trevor Gordon and the Bee Gees. None of the records made a noticeable dent in the Australian charts, but there was one very intrigued listener.

The first record business person to take an active interest in the Bee Gees was Bill Shepherd, an English arranger who had emigrated to Australia. He was the first to see the potential of the group, and as a producer at Festival, he began to do something about it. Barry notes that Bill "saw that there was more to us than other people thought there was and said, 'I want to produce you.' He talked Fred Marks into letting him produce us."

Maurice recalls the night that Bill sneaked them into the studio to record "Wine and Women." Festival wasn't interested in releasing or recording any more Bee Gees material, but, according to Maurice, "Bill took 'Wine and Women' to them and said, 'This is the last track the boys did.' And they said, 'We may as well release it.' That was the start of our new sound."

It was supposed to be their last record, but "Wine and Women," released in July of '65, was destined to be a hit, even if it took a bit of behind the scenes skullduggery for it to reach the charts. Barry begins the tale. "Robin had drawers stacked full of charts. We figured it out, with our expertise on the charts . . . how many records you had to sell to get into the top 40." Barry points out that "we hadn't had a hit, and we weren't going to get a hit. As far as we were concerned, we were going to make it one way or another. We didn't know when it was going to be. We just kept making records, and looking at each other and saying, 'One day, this one's going to be a hit. This is going to be the one,'" Robin admits that "we were very desperate to get a record in the charts. First of all, we found out the shops of the radio station's survey . . . Walton's, Woolworth's, about six in all. That's all we needed. You don't have to sell very many records to get on the actual Sydney charts. We arranged for our fan club to meet us on the steps of Sydney Town Hall. It wasn't hard to see them, to rendezvous with them 'cause there was only six of them. We met them with our two hundred dollars, and we gave them money to go around to those shops." Barry elaborates further. "We knew if we could sell 400 records on that Saturday afternoon, by the next Wednesday chart, we'd be at #35. We only had $200 so it could be no higher than 35. Sure enough, the next week, the record was 35 with a bullet. We were going to get there eventually, but we had to find a way to make it happen and we did."

"Once it got in the top forty," Robin notes, "we didn't have to worry any further because the radio station would pay attention to it. Then the record has to take care of itself. The play is there, but play doesn't necessarily sell records. If they like the record, they'll go out and buy it, but they can't buy it unless they

37

hear it." "Wine and Women" reached #19 in the charts, but, as Barry recalls, "it did an enormous amount for us. It made momentum for us in the country, 'cause people were starting to know about the Bee Gees, even if it wasn't very much. Even if it was just one hit, it was something."

The Bee Gees had their hit, but they still had the old problem of playing to adult audiences. Now in their teen years, they were really itching to play more rock 'n' roll type music. Hugh recalls, "We did a club once, a returned soldiers audience, mostly in their forties and fifties. They did the usual act, got the acclaim. Barry came over and said, 'They don't want this, you know. They wand to rock.' I said, 'Get off. Look at the ages of them.' The second spot, Maurice put on his electric guitar, and they started rocking. The bloody place is jumping . . . the old geezers' feet were going." All of the brothers were becoming musicians, and they began to incorporate their new talent into the act. Maurice explains that he "used to play guitar in our act, a little lead. I love the bass because it always used to add depth . . . thicken out what we'd already sung. I got more interested in the bass than anything else. Guitar was first, piano was second and bass was third." Robin was also playing keyboards by now, but most of the Bee Gees instrumental skills were directed towards composing and record making. When it came time to perform, it was still mostly the three of them harmonizing around Barry's guitar. Barry feels "that we continued to work to adults and that's where our damage was done, why we'd never really made it as a pop group earlier. You've got to be visible to the kids. You've got to be there all the time, and we weren't doing that."

Their nightclub act had always played on their little boy cuteness, but while their act hadn't changed much, the brothers had. They were teenagers now, and because they were surrounded by adults so much of the time, they tended to be older than their years. Maurice claims that "sexually, even physically, we advanced a lot quicker, hairy chests and so forth. We never flaunted the fact that we had a great sex life." Barry was quite a ladykiller. "When I was about fifteen or sixteen, I got myself engaged to about six girls at one time. My sex life was amazing for about six months until they all found out. You really have to keep one away from the others at all times. It works boys, but don't push your luck. I wasn't very nice to my girlfriends." Robin remembers that he "fell in love all the time. My first love was a girl called Margaret, and she lived in a place called Lidcombe in Sydney." Ever the romantic, Robin adds, "We screwed every night."

The Bee Gees were growing up fast because, as Maurice points out, "we were adults all our lives. I suppose we were a bit outspoken on a few occasions, and naturally people thought we were a bit obnoxious 'cause we just talked to them like an adult. And they'd think, "Ooo, big-headed little obnoxious bugger.' My dad used to say 'They think you're obnoxious little brats.' I never knew what the word obnoxious meant anyway, so I just went, 'Hey great, we're obnoxious.'

"We grew up on television, like the Osmonds did, and the Australians watched us grow. We were well known in Australia as moms' and dads' favorites. We'd come on TV and they'd say. 'Those three little kids again. Aren't they lovely? Aren't they cute?' I think people used to call us obnoxious little brats because we were successful and their kids weren't."

Barbara feels that her sons "were precocious at times because they were mixing with older people all the time, but they were nice with it. They weren't cheeky. To this day, none of them have ever answered me back. They never would. They make fun or make little jokes, but they never answered us back or questioned us." Sometimes, in earlier years, the boys did go too far. Maurice remembers "one day we were walking down this road in Surfer's Paradise. I'd heard a joke that I had to tell. It was just Barry and my father, and I was in the middle of them. The tag line of the joke was, 'Yes, you silly C- -t.' I didn't know what that meant; I just thought it was cute. My dad turned around and belted me across the head, gave me a thick ear. I said, 'What's wrong? Didn't you laugh?' And Barry went, 'Come here you fool. Do you know what that meant?' I said 'No, but it made everybody laugh.' He told me what it meant, and that's the only time, the first and last time, I ever swore. There was one other time. We were driving to a gig, and some idiot sped past us and a police car was chasing this fellow. As he went around the corner, the guy jumped the curve. This other guy on the pavement almost jumped three feet in the air 'cause he was so scared. I said, "Bloody hell. Looks like it knocked the shit out of him.' I got another clout across the ear because I'd said 'shit.' We were never allowed to swear. That's one thing my father really stood strongly for. When you're a kid, you don't respect your elders. Now that we're family men, I would hate to see my child answer me back. Until you have children of your own, you don't know what your parents go through. Then you realize they were a blessing—what they must have gone through with us being five kids. Fortunately, three of us and dad were on the same wavelength regarding the business. Even then, my father treated us like, 'You're my kids, don't answer me back, even if you do work and support the family.' The most important thing he taught was respect for elders, even though we were the money earners. Thank God he did."

Following up a hit record proved troublesome for the Bee Gees, and "I Was A Lover, A Leader of Men" wasn't a hit. It did draw considerable attention to the

40

group anyway because the song earned Barry the "Composer of the Year" award from Adelaide's Radio 5KA in 1965. Still, the Gibbs hadn't really earned the respect of their record company. Their five year contract had three years remaining, and there wasn't a great desire on Festival's part to continue releasing Bee Gees records. An LP, the Bee Gees first, was released in Novmber of 1965, and it was called **The Bee Gees Sing and Play 14 Barry Gibb Songs.** Other than that LP, Festival was reluctant to push the group. A final Festival single, "Cherry Red," failed to chart, and it looked like their relationship with Festival was over.

It was March of 1966. The Bee Gees, according to Hugh, had firm offers from both RCA and EMI, and they were ready to make the switch. Festival, though, wouldn't let them out of their contract. This led to a flaming row one day between Hugh and Barry on one side and Fred Marks on the other. The shouting could be heard ringing up and down the corridors at Festival. As Barbara recalls, "They still talk about this in muted tones at Festival." Ultimately, however, the Bee Gees weren't released from their contract, but were instead sublet to Spin Records which was run by Nat Kipner. Hugh feels that this was just "Festival's way of getting the Bee Gees out of the way."

While Nat Kipner believed the Bee Gees could be successful, it was a man named Ossie Byrne who really turned the group's fortunes around. Byrne had a tiny studio in the back of his butcher shop in the Sydney suburb of Hurtsville, and he allowed the Bee Gees to record there for free. Robin remembers that Ossie had "always been a fan of ours but thought that we should have been handled a bit better, so he said, 'Come to my studio; you can have all the time you want.' And we were in there day and night, and we could experiment for the first time. We felt great. Wrote all our own music. It was like a whole new door had been opened." Barry explains that this opportunity to record for hours on end "was what we wanted. He was like a spirit guide, sent to make sure that what we wanted to do happened. He wanted to help us develop." According to Robin, "Ossie said, 'Your greatest enemy has been that no one has ever given you studio time.' So we said, 'All we want is to go in there for two months. If we put time in the studio, we can bring out a number one record.' We knew that, so we went in there."

It was the summer of 1966 that the Bee Gees spent their studio apprenticeship in Ossie's studio, learning not only how to make records but also discovering that given the time and opportunity they could be prolific songwriters as a team as well as individually. It was also at this time that they began to realize that they wanted to leave Australia. Barry remembers that "the three of us and Ossie said, 'We've got to get out of here in order to do it.' We discussed it over a period of weeks, and then we went and told our parents how we felt. Mom and Dad were unhappy to pull up stakes knowing that where they'd come from wasn't all that great." Hugh recalls "being against it at first. I thought it'd be too fierce." At one point, he even threatened to take away the boys' passports, but eventually understood his sons were determined to leave. Barry remembers how his parents tried to discourage them saying, " 'Chances are no one will want to know you. Chances are you'll want to come back.' The brothers countered by saying, 'We know, but if we don't try, we'll hate each other all our lives for not pushing each other into it.' Eventually, after a few arguments and reappraisals and everything, we decided to leave for England."

Between that decision and the Gibbs' departure in January of 1967, the Bee Gees ironically had the success in Australia they had so long sought. "Spicks and Specks," one of the many songs recorded at Ossie

Byrne's studio, was released as a single in September of 1966 and became a big hit all over the country. Barry notes that "we proved something to ourselves that given the time and inspiration from other people, we were able to do a lot of things. But we had to get to England because it was the doorway to international success. Australia could not give us that." In examining their Australian career, Robin feels that "we never had many highlights considering how the Bee Gees were treated at that time. If we would have had any highlights in our professional career, we may have even stayed. But the way we were treated, the only remedy for the Bee Gees was to leave Australia."

Just as they were getting ready to say good-bye, Australia was finally beginning to say hello. In '66, they were voted Group of the Year and Barry won the country's top songwriter award from the national press. At 17, Barry already had an impressive history as a composer. Hugh recalls that one writer wondered "how it is possible for a boy of 17 to write such songs when he's never experienced these emotions. He wrote such deep love songs." By late '66, Barry had written songs that were recorded by such Australian singers as Col Joye, Ronnie Burns, Lonnie Lee, Reg Lindsay and Noleen Batley, and rock groups The Twilights, The Vibrants and Steve & The Board. The latter group was led by Steve Kipner, the son of Nat Kipner. That group's drummer at one time included a young man by the name of Colin Petersen, a future Bee Gee.

With "Spicks and Specks" climbing the charts, the Bee Gees 2nd Australian LP, **Monday's Rain,** was re-released with the hit included as the new title cut. The album consisted largely of material recorded with Ossie, songs which were group's first recordings that are enjoyable to this day. The group sent that album (and tapes of other songs from those sessions, tunes like "Mrs. Gillespie's Refrigerator," "Deeply Deeply Me"

43

and "Gilbert Green") to a number of management companies in England. Included on their mailing list was NEMS, the organization that was run by one Brian Epstein, manager of the Beatles.

Before leaving Australia, the Bee Gees also finally threw away their Brylcream and grew their hair. "Just before we left," Barbara remembers, "Hugh allowed them to let their hair grow long. They'd been pestering him for a long time." Hugh asked his sons at the time, "Does it make you sing better when your hair is long?" Of a more serious nature, all the Bee Gees didn't escape Australia as bachelors. Barry "met Maureen Bates in Sydney along with her parents at a Returned Soldiers' League club. We went steady at sixteen, and then tied ourselves into a marriage which I don't think either of us wanted. I think she just wanted the security. We were leaving Australia and going to England. She didn't want to face the situation of waiting for me to come back and thinking that I might not. She put me in a position of, 'Let's get married now, before you go.' It started off well enough, but where it had worked as boyfriend and girlfriend, it didn't work once the words of marriage had been pronounced. It became a prison after that for both of us. It caused her far more distress than it caused me." The marriage ended in separation after little more than a year, and officially died in divorce in 1970.

There had been one other addition to the Gibb family before they left: Leslie had given birth to a daughter, Bernice. So when the Gibbs left Australia for England, their group numbered seven: Hugh, Barbara, Maurice, Robin, Barry, Andy and Ossie Byrne. Another Gibb friend, Bill Shepherd, had already moved back to England. Leslie remained behind with her husband, Keith Evans, although they moved to England later in 1967 where they remained for a few years before returning permanently to Australia.

One thing the Bee Gees did not do before leaving Australia was to make a big deal of their departure. They had watched a number of Australian acts leave for England and "the big time" with huge send-offs and newspaper headlines predicting that this was the act that would make it big around the world. Nobody, with the exception of the Seekers, had enjoyed any lasting success, so the Bee Gees sort of sneaked out. As Maurice admits, "We knew that if we didn't do it in England, we could always come back to Australia and still work. We never went off with a big bang. No one knew we left." Hugh recalls how he insisted that there be no ballyhoo. "We sent postcards to DJs from the first stop on the trip which was Thursday Island. The cards said, "We're on our way to England."

The Gibb family, plus and minus a couple of different members, was making the return half of a journey that had begun in 1958. While they had found a pleasant way of life "Down Under," the ambitions of the Bee Gees dictated a return to the Mother Country. Unfortunately, their financial condition was much the same as when they had left Manchester in '58. It was the money earned from the success of "Spicks and Specks" that paid for part of the trip. Hugh worked out the details of the rest. "We found out that the Seekers had worked their way over to England on a ship called the 'Fair Sky.' We didn't have the money for passage, so we did a deal with the ship lines. The boys and I were to travel free, and in return, we were supposed to entertain on the boat."

At the moment of the group's departure, an event took place that epitomized the treatment they'd received all along from Festival Records. "Festival," Robin remembers, "brought an injunction to try and stop us leaving the country. Festival Records who once said, 'Change your name and move to Melbourne.' Festival Records who once said, 'Forget it fellas, if you can't do it here, what makes you think you can do it anywhere else.' And Festival Records who once said, 'Quit, it's finished.' It hadn't even started, and they said it's finished.' " It was a bitter note on which to end their Australian stay, but it was that kind of treatment that allowed the Bee Gees to leave with a firm resolve of "we'll show you." It wasn't until they were on the ship that they learned that "Spicks and Specks" had gone to number one. Robin recalls feeling that "this was a sign. We knew why it was number one, because people like Ossie had taken the time to help us. If Festival had taken the time, it wouldn't have been so frustrating, but we had to do it ourselves in the end." The brothers also were quite secure in the feeling that if they didn't make it as a pop group, they could always make it as songwriters. As Robin notes, "We all wrote our own materials, and we were always interested in being top songwriters. It had always been our main goal."

The treatment that the Bee Gees received in Australia was one of the key reasons for leaving. It really isn't possible to exaggerate the bitterness and frustration that they felt. The Brothers Gibb considered themselves to be worthy of a fair hearing by the public, and they feel they never got that. Even after they left, Barry notes, the sniping didn't end. "When we were on the boat, we'd keep getting reports from friends about 'Spicks and Specks' becoming a hit while we were on the way to England. The local Australian papers had stories like, 'Bee Gees Abandon Australia.' I thought that was unfair."

Leaving a dead-end success in Australia behind, the Brothers Gibb headed home to England and an uncertain future. They left behind a very certain life as successful Australian stars. Yet there really was no choice. The group had to leave if they were to be true to themselves. "Col Joye was the only chap in Australia that said to me, 'Hughie, you've got the only act here that'll make it overseas.' He was the only one ever said it." It would only take the Bee Gees a few months to prove Col Joye correct and the rest of the Australian music industry wrong.

3

ENGLAND
& STARDOM

Barry: "Our mother reads the cards. Before we left Australia she said, 'I can't tell whether it'll be five years or five months, but within five you will have what you want, within five months of your arriving in England.' She told us about Robert [Stigwood] before we met him. She said, 'A sort of middle-aged blond man will come into your life'." Barbara Gibb's predictions all came true, but it took more than a feeling.

On January 3, 1967, six Gibbs and Ossie Byrne left Australia on the "Fair Sky." Hugh recalls that the first day aboard, he went to the purser, according to Hugh, "didn't even know we were aboard or that we were supposed to perform. All the entertainment plans had been made. So he said, 'Well, if we have a ball some night, would the boys mind doing twenty minutes?' I said that would be all right." Hugh was quite relieved because he "had visualized their performing every night, and that they would go through all their material. In five weeks, they only appeared three or four times."

Those performances, however, were a portent of things to come. "The boat was full of young Australians going to England," Hugh recalls. "They knew the Bee Gees, and the boys got a fantastic reception. They did twenty minutes of their night club act, and then Maurice would plug his electric guitar in. And they'd start doing rock 'n' roll. The place would be packed. Barry's fingers would be bleeding; he never used a pick. They'd do 'Twist and Shout.' They found that if they did Beatles' stuff, the crowd went mad." Along those lines, Maurice recalls that when the ship stopped in Ceylon, he bought a sitar, "and when I walked out with it everyone was yelling, 'George. Beatles.' I went, 'No, sorry. He's got more hair than me'. That day, we learned 'Norwegian Wood' [a song on the Beatles' **Rubber Soul** LP on which George Harrison had introduced the sitar to rock music]. We practiced like mad on the boat coming over, sat on a few cushions. The sitar was the first thing I sold when we got back to England."

It was during this voyage that the brothers, especially Robin, indulged in their passion for storytelling. Maurice remembers how "every day, the day's activities would be posted in a glass case, and alongside the list of activities, in the corner of the case, there always used to be a poem by the phantom poet of the 'Fair Sky.' And no one knew who it was. It was Robin, typing away on a little typewriter down in our cabin. All these little poems like 'The Little House on the Hill.'

The little house on the hill
Where it was all red
With a lovely red fence all around it
And it blew up

And it would just go on. He'd carry on with a stupid load of rubbish poetry. And everyone got fascinated by this guy."

And every day, Robin would stand off to the side, with a shy, sly grin and watch people read his poems, all the time knowing the secret of the phantom poet of the "Fair Sky." During that trip, Robin and Barry also wrote an entire book of short stories. There were once plans to publish them, but along with many of the

Gibbs' ideas, it wasn't realized due to the internal problems the group would experience in the late '60s.

The journey back to England took five weeks. In an adventurous spirit, the Gibb and Ossie Byrne got off the boat when it reached Suez and went by land to Cairo. They traveled through the Sahara Desert by bus, saw the Ancient Pyramids and joined the ship at Port Said. They later visited Pompeii and Naples.

After an absence of almost nine years, the Gibb family arrived in England on February 7, 1967 when the "Fair Sky" reached the docks at Southampton. The Gibbs' first stopping place, Hugh remembers, "was a grotty [grotesque] hotel in Hampstead. That Friday, we rented a furnished, semi-detached [two-family] house in Hendon." A discouraging week or two went by as the Bee Gees tried to find work in England. Hugh recalls that "people in Australia sent one or two letters on our behalf. The Seekers' manager, Eddie Jarret, was in the offices of Sir Lew Grade, the Grade Organization, the big management complex. 'Very interested' he says," until the Bee Gees actually got to England and went to see him at his office at the Palladium. According to Hugh, "He painted a rather glum picture. He knew the pop scene and said, 'There's nothing there.' 'Spicks and Specks' didn't mean a thing to him. He said, 'I'll try to get some club work for you boys, try to keep you working.' That was that, so we went back home."

Meanwhile, at the Gibbs' home in Hendon, a mysterious Mr. Stickweed had been trying to get in touch with the Bee Gees all day long. Hugh said, "Stickweed? I don't know who he is." Barbara replied, "I don't know either, but if he doesn't ring tonight, he'll call you again tomorrow." Hugh remembers thinking that the mysterious Mr. Stickweed was "one of Eddie Jarret's bookers with some club work for us." At twenty of eight the next morning, everyone was still in bed when the phone rang. It was Mr. Stickweed. The entire family gathered around the phone as Hugh listened. "He says, 'My name is Robert Stigwood, Brian Epstein's partner.'" The boys were on the stairs and they say, "Who is it?" As Hugh romantically remembers, he triumphantly whispered, "It's Eppie!" meaning Brian Epstein. It was certainly close enough. Mr. Stigwood continued. "Look, we've been doing a lot of reshuffling in the office here, and we've just come across the acetate you sent us, and we played it. Could you come along and see us this afternoon?" "I said, 'Fine. You want to see the boys?' 'By all means, please bring them along.' That's how it all started."

For over ten years, Robert Stigwood has been the Bee Gees' manager, and he recalls the chain of circumstances that brought him together with the Gibbs. "I was the joint manager and director of NEMS with Brian. They sent an acetate and song tapes, and I heard them. I couldn't believe their harmony singing and their songwriting. So, I discovered they were on a boat, and they didn't leave me any address where they were going to be in England. I think I tracked them down almost the day after they arrived and invited them to come into the office and have a meeting with me. And they came in. They were incredibly funny characters. Amusing. Often, when people are just starting up in the business, they're fairly nervous when they meet managers. I was amazed at their relaxation. They were polite, but totally relaxed, cracking lots of gags. We used to have a lot of fun because I loved their humor. Apart from launching their career, we all became very good friends. The personalities you see today are exactly the same as they were back then."

Molly Hullis, who is now also Mrs. Robin Gibb, was the receptionist at NEMS and remembers the momentous meeting. "They arrived late one afternoon, very bedraggled looking, very old-fashioned clothes as far as

51

England was concerned. I thought, 'Oh, another group to contend with.' They were all sort of terribly shy and nervous and didn't know how to conduct themselves. So I said, 'Who do you want to see?' They said, 'We've come to see Robert Stigwood. We're the Bee Gees'."

After a short chat with "Mr. Stickweed," the Bee Gees found themselves giving their first English "concert." Robert "wanted to see what they sounded like live before we had completed all the contracts. I told them not to get nervous about it. It was just a formal thing I wanted to go through." A taxi was dispatched to Hendon to pick up the Bee Gee guitars, and everyone gathered in the basement of the Saville theatre, the theatre that had been used to film the concert sequences for the Beatles' "A Hard Day's Night." Robert picks up the story: "I'd been to a party the night before and had been up all night, so I came with a dreadful hangover. They thought I wasn't enjoying their music, and I explained that it wasn't that at all, that I really thought they were terrific."

The audition itself just wasn't a smash. Barry recalls that "we did about three or four songs including 'Puff the Magic Dragon,' a Peter, Paul and Mary segment. It concluded with Maurice kissing Robin on the cheek. It used to be very funny. As you get older, it's no longer funny," Barry jokes. "It's highly suspicious and shouldn't be repeated. Robert saw it for what it was. With his hangover and all, he looked terrible and felt terrible. His people sort of walked him out." The Gibbs returned home to an anxious Barbara who asked, "How did it go?" "Don't know," they replied. "He just got up and walked out before we were finished." Hugh recalls saying, "We better go back to Australia." It wasn't all that bleak. As Maurice remembers, when "he left, he said, 'Be at my office at 5.' We went there and Ringo walked out and we almost freaked."

The biggest moment in the Gibbs' young lives was

about to take place. According to Barry, Stigwood said, "We're prepared to offer you a five year contract." Robert calls it a "a pretty standard contract. I often took contracts with artists for one year with options to extend, but the deal I made with them was a firm five year deal." With incredible speed and with no more than his business intuition, Robert Stigwood had in one day met, auditioned and signed three young men who were to become one of the most popular and successful songwriting teams and pop groups since the Beatles. The entire experience was a dream come true, and it was really a million to one shot. When one realizes how many demonstration records and tapes are made and sent out every day, it is staggering to think that a struggling Australian group sent a bunch of their songs to the company managing the Beatles and ended up with a five year contract. The Gibbs had arrived in England with only a few hundred pounds in their pockets; within three weeks, they had signed an exclusive management deal that was to make them millionaires.

With all the excitement, there were two unanswered questions; the first remains a mystery to this day. When the Bee Gees sent their tapes to NEMS, they didn't include an English address because they had no idea where they would be. Nobody knows how Robert got their phone number. Barbara, though, points out that "he's so shrewd, so quick, that he immediately found out where we were. Robert can find anybody if he wants to; he's that type of man." The other question of interest was how Robert came to hear their tapes. According to Barry, "Brian and Robert were sitting around one night, and they had these tapes lying around and said, 'Let's just play them and see what's on them before we dump them.' And they were our tapes." Barbara recalls that "Robert told me that the acetates were on Eppie's desk, and he said to Robert, 'By the way, are you interested in listening to this? It's

53

good, but I'm too busy with the Beatles. You ought to listen to it.' Robert took it home with him, and it was laying on his desk for two-three weeks. One night, when he was doing nothing, he just sat there and listened. And he was knocked out." Robert explains that he "thought with their harmony singing, that natural quality that you only get with brothers, and with their writing ability, it would be very difficult for them to go wrong."

The actual singing took place on February 24, 1967. At a press conference that day, Robert Stigwood said, "The Bee Gees put on one of the most exciting stage shows I've ever seen. They have tremendous versatility, and unbelievable professionalism. It is impossible to overstate their international potential both as performers and composers." The publicity machine was started to spread the word about this great new group; at the same time, Polydor released "Spicks and Specks." It made no noise in England, but was a minor hit in some Western European countries and helped pave the way for future big success. As for the Bee Gees, their few weeks of unemployment in England were over very quickly. Maurice remembers, "Robert told us later that Brian had his boys, and he wanted his Beatles. Really, the songs were what he was after, our songwriting. So it was just 'Go!' He said, 'Can you be in the studio next Friday to start recording your first album?' " If ever there was a question the Bee Gees wanted to hear, that was the one.

So the Brothers Gibb went to Polydor Studios to write songs and record song demos before moving on to the main studios at IBC. It was at Polydor that the Bee Gees were to write their first international hit. Through the years, the brothers have always sought out places to sing that have great echo, whether it was a bathroom or a hallway or a recording studio. Barry recalls that "we were on the back steps at Polydor

Records, next to an elevator. The staircase went around the elevator for about four floors, and there was a lot of echo. It was very dark, and it was night. We couldn't see each other. But the echo was amazing. It just inspired us to write that song. Inspiration also came from the Aberfam Mining Disaster [in Wales] which happened at the same time."

"That song" was "New York Mining Disaster 1941," a haunting ballad that was the absolute perfect song with which to launch the group. And like much of the group's early British work, "Mining Disaster" was similar to the sound of a very popular act. Barry admits, "We were basically influenced by the Beatles above everything else. A few of our songs were direct influences of the Beatles' music."

To the brothers, one of the most exciting aspects of recording **Bee Gees 1st** was that they were able to use strings. "In Australia," Barry explains, "what we really wanted to hear was strings, but we couldn't get that there. So when we got to England, we knew that we wanted to hear our music with an orchestra behind it. Robert asked us what we wanted to do with our music, and we asked him for an orchestra." While many pop groups have incorporated strings in their albums, the Bee Gees were the first to really use the orchestra as an integral part of their music as opposed to strings being used to "sweeten" the sound. And even though they have no formal music training, the brothers, as Robin notes, do "all our own string arrangements. We'd sit down with the tape recorder with the backtrack of the song we'd previously recorded, play it, and we'd hum along the string lines we'd want to hear. It was like composing a separate song, but it's still composing. We have someone write down the dots for us." From 1967-1973 that someone was Bill Shepherd, one of the few music business people from Australia that had faith in the Bee Gees. Barry remembers that "we always wanted strings on our albums. When we met Bill Shepherd and found out he was a string arranger, we said, 'Will you come back to England with us?' We never thought about his abilities. We never really have. People always clicked with us or didn't." When Robert Stigwood told the Bee Gees they could use strings, the person they called was Bill Shepherd. Throughout their career, family has always been of paramount importance and that hasn't just included blood relations. Bill Shepherd had believed in the Bee Gees in Australia, had furthered their career, and the Gibbs hadn't forgotten. Like a select few "believers," Bill Shepherd was part of the Bee Gees extended family for many years, arranging strings on their albums and conducting the orchestra in concert.

Of course, another old Australian pal who was in the studio with the group was Ossie Byrne. As co-producer of **Bee Gees 1st,** it is hard to determine his contribution to that record, but Ossie's contribution to the Bee Gees first big success can not be underestimated. A third Australian joined the team shortly after Bill Shepherd. In the same apartment building that Shepherd lived was a young drummer, Colin Petersen. Colin was a child actor, best known for his starring role in the film "Smiley," but he was an accomplished drummer who had been in many Aussie groups, notably Steve and The Board. Bill brought Colin to the Bee Gees, and he was hired.

It was during the late winter weeks of 1967 that the Bee Gees "first" international career was taking shape at an accelerating speed. At that time, for the only time in their career, the Bee Gees considered changing their name. Robin: "We told Robert we'd like to change our name to 'Rupert's World.' He looked at us very strange. It wasn't so bad a name for 1967. In those days, the names didn't last very long, just as long as they're in fashion. So he said, 'We'll bring out your first record under the Bee Gees and if it stiffs, then we'll change your name and no one will know.' " As Barry recalls, "It was like changing your name from Charlie Shit to Fred Shit."

Back in the studio, the Bee Gees were rapidly completing work on their LP. With the exception of "Mining Disaster," "Holiday," and "Every Christian Lion Hearted Man Will Show You," all the songs had been written either in Australia or on the boat ride over so it only took three weeks to record the album. The songs are full of ideas that were spilling from the young Gibbs' fertile imaginations. Where they had once been mostly content to write love songs or ordinary story songs, Barry and Robin, especially Robin, were beginning to create some rather unusual fantasies. "Mining Disaster" was the first step in that direction.

One of the first records the Bee Gees heard upon their return to England was the Beatles' "Strawberry Fields Forever." The effect of that record on the Bee Gees in terms of visual imagery and sounds was considerable. On **Bee Gees 1st,** the sound of the mellotron, a newcomer to rock on "Strawberry Fields. . . ," became part of the Bee Gees sound.

In April of 1967, Robert Stigwood began to prepare the public for the arrival of a "new Beatles." Of course, he did it in a very clever, albeit expensive way. With a mammoth party at a London discotheque, and a publicity campaign that cost thousands of dollars, Stigwood released "NY Mining Disaster 1941" with the footnote that here was a group that was heir apparent to the Beatles. In Robert's usual modest fashion, he recently said, "I did a very big launch on them initially." At the time, if the word hype had been in use, it would have applied perfectly. With tremendous hoopla, Stigwood attached the Bee Gees new music to the Beatles' coat tails. Regardless of how favorable or unfavorable the comparisons proved to be, Stigwood accomplished within days what it often takes years for other groups to do. He had the entire British music world talking about the Bee Gees. Nobody knew anything about them, but that didn't matter. Tongues were wagging, and their English career was underway.

During the recording of **Bee Gees 1st,** a young man with a problem had gone to visit Robert Stigwood. Dick Ashby was road manager of a British group called the Birds, and when that group disbanded, Ashby found himself with a van full of equipment but nobody to play the instruments. When he told Stigwood of his predicament, Stigwood immediately bought the "gear and tackle" and hired Ashby to be the Bee Gees road manager. Ashby has been with the Bee Gees ever since, becoming their day-to-day personal manager in 1970. Today, he is the key liaison between the Bee Gees and the world.

Ashby recalls the Bee Gees earliest British concerts with a smile and a shake of his head. "We did some club dates, sometimes two clubs a night. I remember doing the Nottingham Boat House and the Nottingham Beachcomber both in one night. I was handling all the equipment by myself. The Bee Gees weren't known at the time, 'Mining Disaster' was just breaking, so the crowd reaction was virtually nil. It was a little bit better than a bar band because Robert had started his campaign, started splashing his money around, so they knew who they were seeing, even if they didn't have the faintest idea what they were listening to. The audience knew the name was beginning to mean something." It didn't mean much because, as Barry recalls, "we had to do nearly an hour of everybody else's material because no one knew our stuff. And we had 'Mining Disaster,' so that was our show. At the Nottingham Boat House, our dressing room was filled with a foot of water."

The Bee Gees' first appearance in England outside

of nightclubs and bars was as part of the Easter week show at London's Saville Theatre where they had auditioned for a hungover Robert Stigwood. This time, Barry remembers, their reception was even worse. "Vince Melouney joined us as our lead guitarist, and we had one afternoon for rehearsal. They had us on a rock 'n' roll bill, and we'd just formed the group and it wasn't really ready. We hadn't even worked out a show. It was the first time in our lives we were a band. Up to then, it had just been the three of us with a guitar. We had a four hour rehearsal with Vince and Colin, went onstage and they hated us."

It wasn't the Bee Gees the audience hated. It was anybody that delayed the arrival of the man they'd come to see, Fats Domino. Gerry and the Pacemakers were also appearing, and they'd had a bunch of hits, but nobody really wanted to see them either. Barry points out that "all they wanted was Fats Domino. They were all Teddy Boys and hated us. Robin got an egg thrown at him that hit him right in the chest." That show obviously isn't one of Robin's favorite topics for what he would call a "chin wag," but he did try and explain the crowd's hostility. "You see, musically, our direction was very scattered then. We didn't know what our image would be or who we would appeal to. It was a very heavy rock 'n' roll audience. We had to sing something rock 'n' roll; otherwise they would have thrown knives at us instead of eggs."

That day, the Bee Gees' act included their Peter, Paul and Mary segment as well as versions of Cream's "Strange Brew," "You Keep Me Hanging On" and "High-Heeled Sneakers." Robin feels "It was just wrong for us to have sung 'Puff the Magic Dragon' to a heavy rock 'n' roll audience. It would have been wrong for Peter, Paul and Mary to have walked on stage in front of a crowd like that. That show was wrong for us. We weren't heavy rock 'n' roll." But the Bee Gees can't blame rock 'n' roll for the eggs. As Barry half laughingly remembers, "Robin's always been prone to egg-throwing. That was just the second time an egg was accurate on Robin. The other was in Toowoomba, near Brisbane." Dick Ashby has only one memory of the whole event, of "Robin getting hit by an egg, and he carried on with this thing dripping down him." The conditions weren't the best, but the ever-professional Bee Gees finished their program. It was one of the first and last times they ever had trouble winning an audience over.

On April 14, 1967, Polydor released the first "made in England" Bee Gees record, "New York Mining Disaster 1941" b/w "I Can't See Nobody." "In those days," Barry notes, "the only way to sell a group was to say they were the next Beatles, or that it was going to beat the Beatles. The publicity became the comparison. Robert originally said, 'THE MOST SIGNIFICANT TALENT SINCE THE BEATLES.' That was printed everywhere. And that frightened us to death because how can we live up to such a statement?" Frightening or not, once the campaign began and the record was released, the Bee Gees became part of a snowball of publicity that, in Robin's words, "was overwhelming then. But when I look back, it was more of a big publicity thing then a big record sales thing. It was a great angle, very shrewd publicity on Robert Stigwood's behalf. The guy was and is a genius for timing. In those days, Robert's help was invaluable." As for the comparison to the Beatles, Maurice says that "it's an honor. Those guys have done more for this business than anyone." To Robin, "At that time, it was flattery, sort of, and at that time, it was also necessary to expose a new name. What better way than to use the biggest group in the world as a vehicle."

In England, Robert Stigwood compared the Bee Gees to the Beatles. In America, he allowed a lot of people to think the Bee Gees were the Beatles. Robert remembers that after he'd "launched them in England, because of the nature of their particular song, 'NY Mining Disaster,' I found that British radio people kept comparing them to the Beatles. I wanted to really crack America quickly, so I came up with this scheme of just sending out this record, and everyone thought it was the Beatles." Copies of "Mining Disaster" were sent to radio stations and record industry people on records with blank labels. As Maurice recalls, "They played 'Mining Disaster' for about two weeks without saying who it was. They just said it was an English group, and their names begin with a 'B.' Naturally, everyone thought it was the Beatles. And John (Lennon) made it better by denying it." Robert: "And then it was announced, 'No, it's not the Beatles. It's a new group called the Bee Gees.' That was the American launch." Dick Ashby: "I don't know how much Robert spent on that initial campaign; I would think somewhere between £ 30,000-50,000 was spent on that very first launching of **Bee Gees 1st** and 'NY Mining Disaster.' Not a lot of money by today's standards, but for those days, it was an awful lot of money to spend."

"New York Mining Disaster 1941" was a top-twenty hit on both sides of the Atlantic, and made it to number ten in Germany. The often-overlooked flip side of the disk, "I Can't See Nobody," is an important Bee Gees song. This ballad, soulfully sung by Robin, was more than an example of the Bee Gees versatility. It was a very early nod towards the group's favorite music. "Ever since we began," Robin points out, "soul music has been our inspiration and it still is. Black music, to me, is the pulse of music."

If anybody still thought that the Bee Gees and the Beatles were the same group, the Bee Gees second single ended the debate. "To Love Somebody," another stirring, emotion-packed number, was a big hit in the

U.S. and Germany and became the group's first standard, a song that many artists recorded. Maurice notes that "people cut it as soul, people cut it as country, people cut it as R & B. From Janis Joplin to Frank Sinatra, there's some big wild difference there. You could do it any sort of way. The lyrics were very soulful."

While "To Love Somebody" made it into the upper reaches of the charts outside of England, inside it was a different story. Partly, that was due to the arrival of THE musical event of the decade. Barry: "Just before our album came out, Robert brought home **Sgt. Pepper's Lonely Hearts Club Band.** Nobody could believe it. It frightened us to death." Maurice: "It was incredible. He just put in on his stereo and we went, 'Jesus.'" Barry: "Our album was all ready to go. We only wished we could have gone back into the studio after we'd heard their album."

The summer of 1967 was the "Summer of Love" in San Francisco and in the music world it was the summer of **Sgt. Pepper.** That July, the Bee Gees made their first trip to the United States which included their debut American television appearance on Dick Clark's "American Bandstand." That was the only time the brothers performed in America in 1967. The rest of the time, they were either promoting their newly released **Bee Gees 1st** or busy writing songs for their second album. During that trip, they also met Otis Redding, an idol of theirs and a special favorite of Barry's. As a soul singer, Otis had been very influential in forging Barry's vocal style, and it has been said that "To Love Somebody" had been written in hopes that Otis might record it. According to Robin, "Otis was going to record it, but he died in a plane crash before he got a chance."

Like any other tourists on their first trip to New York, the Bee Gees took a scenic cruise through the

New York Harbor. With Manhattan's awesome skyline in the background, the Bee Gees wrote their next single about a nearby place they'd never been to, "Massachusetts." Barry explains, "We were writing a twist on flowerpower because we were getting tired of it long before anybody else did, and we thought why not write about somebody going home who's been to San Francisco and didn't like it." For Maurice, there is a painful memory associated with the song. "It was the last time I saw Brian Epstein . . . a Friday 'cause he was found dead on Sunday. He was supposed to join us in Cannes the next day. He came out of his office and said that 'Massachusetts' is going to be the world's number one. He said, 'It's beautiful' and walked away. That's the last words he ever said to me."

"Massachusetts," the archetypical Bee Gees ballad of their first era, was released as a single in September of 1967. It became their first "monster" hit, going to number one in England, Germany, and many other countries around the world. In America, it made it to number eleven. Worldwide, the record sold five million copies, an extraordinary number in 1967. More than any one record, it was "Massachusetts" that cemented their success. And very much as Barbara Gibb had predicted, it had only taken five months for the Bee Gees to become international stars. And just as quickly, they almost lost two members.

Both Vince and Colin were native Australians and were in England on temporary visas. In the latter half of '67, they were told they would have to leave the country. Robert Stigwood, a master of media manipulation, engineered a "governmental policy change," as he remembers. "I had to take on the British government over that one. I'd just launched the group and they were incredibly successful, but the government told Vince and Colin they couldn't stay in the country any longer. I appealed to the Home Office, and I was turned down. So I thought 'I'll have to use the media, to focus the public and force the government [to change their mind].' So I staged a whole series of events. I had fans chaining themselves to the railings of Buckingham Palace. I marched an elephant on the Home Office in Whitehall, a procession that tied up London's traffic for a day. I landed a helicopter full of fans in the Chancellor of the Exchequer's garden. They ran and assaulted him and told him what a terrible thing it was. I had the Prime Minister's holiday residence picketed. It was in a very remote place, so I flew fans in in helicopters and had them about ten feet from his window with 'Save the Bee Gees' posters. We blew it up so much that in the Home Office itself that dealt with immigration, all the secretaries started putting up 'Save the Bee Gees' posters."

The Brothers Gibb themselves told the British government that rather than see two of their band deported, they would all leave England and settle in America or Spain or Germany. "Finally," Stigwood fondly recalls, "there was such an uproar in the press that the Prime Minister had to intervene, and he declared the Bee Gees a national asset, and Colin and Vince were given their immigration papers."

When Brian Epstein died that summer, the Beatles and the NEMS Organization were rudderless, and Robert Stigwood found himself with two very big groups under his direction. He also had to choose between them. "What happened was that I had an option on the controlling stocks of NEMS which brought the Beatles under my control. At that time, they were dreaming up Apple, and they wanted to keep Stigwood, NEMS and Apple as one big company and for me to run it. But we could never reach agreement on who would hold the controlling shares. And then when John [Lennon] started to talk to me about some of their Apple plans, I really got very nervous . . . especially when they had their famous 'Magic Alex' character in tow." 'Magic Alex' was one of the more bizarre members of the Beatles entourage in those acidy days of 1967, and as Robert notes, " 'Magic Alex' was going to computerize everything, and John told me all I'd have to do was sit behind a desk with a computer and run the business. I started to get even more nervous, so I made the decision, really, to go on my own, take the Bee Gees and Cream with me and focus my efforts on building their careers. 'Magic Alex,' by the way, after a fortune had been spent, came up with one invention . . . a green plastic apple with a transistor radio inside."

The result of Robert's decision was the founding of the Robert Stigwood Organization. As Dick Ashby recounts, "With the aid of monies gotten together by Robert and his accountant, David Shaw [mainly Polydor money], Robert set off by himself and set up RSO with the Bee Gees and Cream, the only assets at that point. Having left NEMS, he was determined that he was going to have a Beatles of his own, and the Bee Gees were it. In those days, Robert gave his total attention to their career. He was a manager in the finest sense of the word. He did everything. He was in the studio with them, traveling with them. He only had the Bee Gees and Cream. Those were his two loves, as it were."

In many respects, 1967 and the first half of '68 was the best of times for the Bee Gees. After years of hard work, their dreams of success had all come true. They were truly international pop stars with all the benefits befitting their status and for the first time, they were able to indulge themselves and begin to live luxuriously. Where their career had robbed them of their teen years they now had the money to become children again. And every day was Christmas. They had success, fame, fortune . . . they had the fans and the press, and they had the record sales. Exciting things were happening all the time. Maurice: "We were doing a concert on one of those turntable stages where one band's playing and the other band on the other side is getting ready. The Merseybeats were playing, and we were getting ready to go on. Dick (Ashby) ran up the stairs and said, 'Massachusetts' has gone to Number One.' And just then the stage started to revolve around, and we just freaked out."

In November of '67, "World" became a top ten hit in England and a number two smash in Germany. Later that month, on November 19th, the Bee Gees played one of the most satisfying concerts of their young career. They returned triumphantly to the Saville Theatre, site of their disastrous English concert debut on the Fats Domino show. This time, with Bill Shepherd conducting a 30-piece orchestra behind them, it was the Bee Gees whose name was in big letters on the marquee. And, as Hugh points out, "To quote the press at the time, 'The streets were blocked all around, like Beatlemania all over again, to see the Bee Gees.'" Barbara remembers that at that show, "We sat in the box with Paul McCartney and Jane Asher. He was raving about the Bee Gees. When we came out after the show, all the girls were outside, and they all pushed past Paul to get to the boys. And Paul said to me. 'Oh well. It's their turn now. We've had our day.'"

The Bee Gees began 1968 with another German #1, "Words." It was a top twenty hit in England, their third straight at home, and a top twenty hit in America, their fifth consecutive release in the States to make the top twenty. "Words" was also to become one of the most covered songs the Brothers Gibb have ever written. Dozens of artists, including Elvis Presley, recorded their version of this breathy ballad. On January 27, 1968, the Bee Gees made their American concert debut in Southern California at the Anaheim Convention

Center. For the two performances, the Bee Gees received the then-astronomical fee of $50,000. As one writer noted, it was "a figure identical to the Beatles' fee for their first Hollywood Bowl concert." Coincidental with their brief American visit, the group's second album, **Horizontal,** was released. Besides the great title track, the LP featured the two hits, "Massachusetts" and "World" as well as a delightful and diverse collection of Gibb tunes and tales.

After returning from America, the Bee Gees embarked on their first concert tour of Germany. By all accounts, it was the wildest tour they ever had. Molly Gibb, who as an employee at NEMS had seen her share of Beatlemania, thinks that "Germany was wilder than the fans in England at the heights of Beatlemania. But I also think the police in Germany antagonized the fans with guard dogs and guns. There was one point where they hosed the kids down to sort of clear them off the street. They were great concerts, very wild." The wildness, though, was especially inappropriate for the sensitive strains of the Bee Gee music. As Barry points out, "for our music, they were too wild. We couldn't get across the messages in the songs." Maurice: "They'd be raving mad, screaming their heads off, and we'd be doing some things with a lovely melody, and they'd be shrieking, 'Barry! Robin!' "

Besides the teeny-bopper screams that often drowned out the singing, the Bee Gees found that the crush of fans often got dangerous. According to one newspaper account, thousands of fans rushed the Bee Gees' arriving plane in Bremen, "trampling over barriers and police with several people injured (including Robin)." This prompted fans in Hamburg to react by covering every inch of the airport with flower petals. In Frankfurt, 7,000 Bee Gees fans greeted the group wearing masks of the various members. The fans in Cologne were under the impression that orange was the group's favorite color so the crowd at the Cologne air-port was dressed from shoes to shirts in orange. Robin was quoted as saying "It gives us something extra to look forward to everywhere we go. We never know what to expect next." Unfortunately for the Bee Gees, not all the Germans were wearing flowers in their hair. Hugh recalls that "every concert was a battle, One time, the boys had to pull me on stage when the fans trampled the barriers. We had to have police escorts all the time just to get away from the hotels." And on more than one occasion, Maurice recalls, the Bee Gees lives were endangered. "Switzerland was the scariest. There were over 5,000 kids at the airport at Zurich. The entire ride to Bern, the kids were waving union jacks. When we got to the hotel, the police weren't there to meet us. And the kids crushed the car. We were inside and the windows were all getting smashed in, and we were on the floor. The driver managed to get the car out of the crowd and out of town. We had a lot of that in Europe. One time, we did four songs, and had to get off the stage. The kids broke the barriers, wrecked the whole stage, smashed all our equipment. We got out in a very big hurry, with a police escort, straight to the airport, on the plane and on to Lon-don." The British fans, not to be outdone, greeted the group with a massive skywriting message. Five planes, one for each Bee Gee, welcomed the group home and spelled each Bee Gee's name in one hundred foot high letters.

The fan hysteria may have peaked at what has been called "the most spectacular concert in rock history." Dick Ashby: "It was the final concert of their third English tour. Robert conceived a whole plan to try and make some noise with the concert." Robert: "It was a particular stage of their career, and I wanted to create a big event." So on March 27, 1968, the Bee Gees played the Royal Albert Hall backed by a sixty-seven piece orchestra, a fifty piece Air Force Band, and a large choir. Robert: "They'd written a song, 'I Have Decided To Join the Air Force.' They did that once through, and then I had the doors of the hall open in all different directions and this Air Force band marched through the audience playing a reprise of the song. I had a choir of forty or fifty planted in the audience for a song called 'Birdie Told Me.' They looked like the audience because there was no equipment around them. When it got to the reprise of the song, I had sound booms produced, and this section of the audience stood up and performed the chorus. Quite a night."

Molly Gibb recalls that night because "it was such a display of showmanship, one of the first stage-managed pop shows. It was the first group ever to have an orchestra on stage . . . very impressive to see the group standing there, sort of young and nervous, because it was the biggest concert they'd ever done at that stage. It really was an incredible show." As Robin drolly describes that evening, "we had everything on there but the Bee Gees. It was like a Roman spectacular, a bit over done. But it was exciting . . . Robert's usual flair for putting on a show."

Within a year of the biggest event of the Bee Gees career, they would split up.

It's also curious that the Bee Gees followed up one of their greatest moments with one of their few flops of the late '60s. Having enjoyed top-ten success with three straight ballads, the Bee Gees decided that the next record should be a bit more of a toe-tapper. "When we started getting hits with ballads like 'Words,'" Robin explains, "we felt a little claustrophobic. We felt people were just fed up with listening to these sort of slushy ballads coming out, which is not what we wanted to do. But people would automatically say yes, release that, because it's a ballad. They iden-

69

tify you with ballads. We got sick in the end." Not as sick as they got when a non-ballad bombed.

The record was "Jumbo" and according to Maurice, "the only time Robert was wrong was when he said release 'Jumbo' as the A-side instead of the flipside, 'Singer Sang His Song.' We thought that was going to be the A-side, but Atlantic convinced Robert, and Robert had been convinced by Vince and Colin 'cause they liked playing a bit more bluesy stuff. Robert said, 'Never again will I let anybody talk me into anything'." "Jumbo" was only a failure in relative terms in England where it made the top thirty. In Germany, it was a top five hit, but it was in America that the record made no impact as it barely charted.

Following that flop, the Bee Gees decided to take a bit of a vacation. Even then, it was hard to escape, as Robin amusingly recounts. "I was having a holiday in Nairobi. Thank you in Nairobi is 'jumbo.' I remember getting off the plane—I was very disappointed that this record's success was nil, and I was getting off the airplane and this big sort of Nairobian came up to me and he took my bags. I tipped him and he said, 'Jumbo.' And I said, 'Don't rub it in'."

According to the British press, "Jumbo's" failure was some sort of signal. One newspaper addressed itself to "the question, have their fans deserted them since the flop of 'Jumbo' and their recent British tour, which was not as warmly received as was expected." The Bee Gees·answered the critics with their biggest hit since "Massachusetts."

"I've Gotta Get A Message To You" was another rousing ballad in the tradition of "Mining Disaster," with a new death twist thrown in. This time, the character singing the song wasn't trapped in a mine. He was buckled into the electric chair. The early Bee Gees albums always had their share of odd songs, from the personal desolation of "Craise Finton Kirk Royal

70

Academy Of Arts" to the bizarre imagery of "Lemons Never Forget." Combining a lyrical quirkiness with Robin's plaintive vocals often produced an emotional sound that was overwhelming. Barry's powerful lead vocals added a solidness to the songs, as if the singer was quite certain of what he was saying. When Robin and Barry began to incorporate vocal interplay, the songs could often take heartbreaking twists and turns. And on top of all that was the three brothers achingly beautiful harmony. On "I've Gotta Get A Message To You," all of these elements came together in a perfect mesh that was very possibly their best single of the '60s. "Message" was the Bee Gees second British #1, their fifth consecutive top five record in Germany and their first top ten record in America.

It had really been an incredible sixteen months for the Bee Gees since returning to England in February of 1967, and along with all the fame and fortune came an incredible array of awards. They were voted "New Musical Express-Best New Group-1967," 'Sixteen Magazine-World's Most Promising Group" and received the Valentine Award as the "World's Brightest Hope." In a very short span of time, they had scored over two dozen number one hits in fifteen different countries. And they won Bravo Magazine's top award, "The Golden Otto." It's interesting to note that with all of the world-wide acclaim, the Bee Gees hadn't made it into the top five in the American charts nor had they even toured the U.S. When they did go stateside for a tour in the summer of '68, the reception was quite disappointing although the tour had one incredible moment at New York's Forest Hills Stadium, on August 10.

"To English people'," Hugh Gibb explains, "New York is tough. If you crack New York, you're in." With that in the back of their minds, the Bee Gees tensely prepared for their first concert in the "Big

Apple." Hugh: "It was raining that night, but the boys went on with a thirty-piece orchestra, did the show and got a fifteen minute standing ovation. It was amazing. Even hardened backstage guys said, 'Sinatra's never got this!' " What was more amazing was the crowd's refusal to allow the rain to dampen their spirits. Throughout much of the hour and a half concert, most of the audience at this outdoor stadium was drenched by a summer storm. Robert Stigwood couldn't believe it. "I don't think one person in the audience moved. I've never seen a reaction at a concert like that. The audience just wouldn't let them off the stage. It was really tremendous to see. Their original breakthrough in the States was the most exciting thing." Maurice remembers that at the point when "we just started 'Holiday,' it started pouring down. The audience didn't move. I noticed out of the corner of my eye, my dad in the corner crying his eyes out while he was watching it. He'd never admit that, but I saw him. He had tears in his eyes. And as soon as we finished the song, the rain stopped. And I went to the mike and said, 'I'd like to thank God for the special effects'."

For the most part, though, in Barry's words, "the first tour of America was a washout. Forest Hills was a nice moment, L.A. as well. I think both shows were papered to an extent. It wasn't a good show musically; we didn't do a good show then. The band was still not a band; we really didn't have the years of playing as a band that makes it work. And all the gigs in between New York and L.A. had to be cancelled. Nobody bought tickets. They tried to make it look good. We spent the time hiding out in L.A. while Robert was juggling the publicity to make it look like we were invading the country. They got Robin to go into the hospital for a couple of weeks and play 'the game.' "

"The game" Barry refers to is one that the Bee Gees management invented and was one that they would play more than once. The "game" only had one rule, and it wasn't a very pleasant one. The only thing the Bee Gees had to do was say nothing. It was announced that most of the tour had to be "postponed" because Robin had been hospitalized due to nervous exhaustion. At least one writer, Harley Madison reporting in Hullabaloo, guessed at the truth. He wrote: "A basic economic fact of touring is that you have to sell tickets to make money. One wonders why Robin Gibb collapsed from nervous exhaustion only hours before the group was to begin the tour. They missed four dates, then Robin had another illness, a relapse, and had to fly back to Britain for a few days of rest. Just more concerts missed or more tickets that didn't get sold?" As Molly admits, "There was no 'nervous exhaustion.' It was just a thing Robin did for the group, a way out of the tour. Whatever anyone said to them, they did it. They didn't know any different then, didn't know anything about the business world. If it's good for the group, then you do it." Dick Ashby: "The bookings were so disastrous that the group hid out. They weren't worried about the American press so much, but they didn't want the British press to find out they hadn't cracked it."

The summer of '68 brought the release of the Bee Gees third British album, **Idea.** It was also their third effort in a little more than a year. **Bee Gees 1st** is widely regarded as a classic, and Barry has a theory as to why that album is considered to be much better than the two that followed. "In those days, we were raw and maybe that's why a lot of our better ideas came out. We weren't so conscious of the public or the records sold because we hadn't sold records. Those characters came out and those thoughts came out which we didn't even know we were thinking. Like 'Turn of the Century' on **Bee Gees 1st.** Why in heaven's name would we be writing about the turn of the century? At our age, it was a little bit weird. We used to get people who were acid trippers come to our doorstep when we were staying in L.A. during that dismal tour. They would knock on the door and say, 'Hey man. I heard these verses, and I know what you mean.' We'd say, 'Do you? Great.' We didn't."

After **Bee Gees 1st,** Barry explains, "the next two albums we wrote, we never really knew what they meant. They became pictures, became lyrics and were set down." By the fourth LP, as Barry recalls, the songs "were obviously becoming more of a strain at that point." To the public, the songwriting was actually the least obvious place that showed strain. It was in the press that the Bee Gees appeared to be coming apart at the seams. As early as the deportation incident, there had been stories about the Bee Gees splitting up. By the fall of 1968, those stories carried quite a bit of substance although the reports of the imminent demise of the Bee Gees seemed quite overblown. For instance, Barry would be quoted as saying, "Sure, I'm leaving the Bee Gees. I'm going into films." On more careful inspection, the reader would find that Barry added, "But it will be at least two years before that happens." Unfortunately, those qualifications didn't help group relations.

Actually, it was Vince Melouney who was the first to quit the group saying that "now is the time I must try my own musical policies." It really was as simple as that. There was no bitter split. Vince just wanted to pursue his blues guitar muse. His sounds never had fit the Bee Gees' music. While the Gibbs were losing one old mate, they were busy in the studio helping another. Trevor Gordon, a singer they had worked with in Australia, had come to England and with Graham Bonnet formed a group called the Marbles. The Gibbs wrote and produced a single for them, "Only One Woman," which was a top-ten hit. What came next was quite unpleasant, Barry recalls. "A thing happened which often happens with us, and that is, if you get to where you are in this business, at this point and you help somebody, they resent you for it later because they don't want to be tied up with what you are. They want to have their own identity, and that's what happened to the Marbles." It was the only hit the Marbles ever had.

That fall, the Bee Gees (minus Vince) went into the studio to record their fourth LP. Originally titled **An American Opera** and then **Masterpeace** (a pun on the American political scene), the double-record was named after one of its strongest cuts, **Odessa.** An ambitious concept, it was also a deliberate effort by the group to expand their audience. Up to that point, they had been, according to Robin, "only getting singles sales, and we wanted to get into the album market. You don't make it until you get into the album market."

When the classic **Bee Gees 1st** had been a more collaborative effort with Ossie Byrne, Robert Stigwood and the group working as a team, by the time the group went into the studio to record **Odessa,** there wasn't much team spirit left. According to Robin, "there was a falling out between Robert and Ossie. Robert wanted more production rights on the songs. As Robert was our personal manager, Ossie had to step down. We really had no say in the matter at the time. We didn't want to see Ossie go, but we'd thrown everything in Robert's court." Robert had been present through **Horizontal** and **Idea,** but, for the most part, they were on their own during the making of **Odessa.** Most of the grandiose ideas that were to be part of **Odessa** were ultimately scrapped because of the growing strife and lack of cooperation among the brothers. The reporters, who had helped create the success of the Bee Gees, seemed to delight in telling of their problems. The articles began to feed upon themselves. One brother would say something and another brother would respond to the press account without first finding out about the accuracy of a quote. So the arguments continued, and the hurting among the brothers grew stronger. For a while, it was impossible to pick up a British rock paper and not read about some negative happening in the Bee Gees camp, and it was obvious that the entire whirlwind of success had completely engulfed the Bee Gees. The brotherhood that had created the Bee Gees magic was being destroyed. The only positive aspect of the entire troubled time is that while the brothers were going their separate ways, none of them was alone. Along the way, each had found a friend and lover to share his life with, someone who helped him enjoy the success and helped even more when the brothers had to bear the pain of the disintegrating relationship.

Robin was first, by virtue of the fact that the woman he married was Molly Hullis, the NEMS receptionist who had greeted the Bee Gees upon their first arrival at the offices. In those early days, Molly recalls, "Robin would come and sit in the reception area and talk. At that time, he was very concerned about the number of late nights I was keeping up. I would only have maybe a couple of hours sleep and get into work the next morning and carry on. One day, Maurice invited me to this party. When I arrived, Maurice was with somebody else. So I thought, 'Ah, nice one here. I'm off.' Robin said to me. 'Don't go. You might just as well stay now that you've got here.' And that was really the first time we went out. We went from the party to a club, and then we started going out on a regular basis." It was certainly not a thing of "love at first sight" on Molly's part. "It was something that sort of grew." Robin, it seems now, was rather lovestruck. Molly: "Robin's a dreamer, a romantic person. Therefore, he would make a situation romantic even if it wasn't. He is very sensitive. People say he's shy, but he's not. He's just very sensitive about everything, whether it's good or bad. And terribly kind and considerate. Not just to me and the family but to strangers. Always concerned, always prepared to take time out to talk to fans. All the brothers are like that."

Molly and Robin lived together for about a year before they married on December 10, 1968. Before that, they went through a harrowing adventure that seemed to typify the Gibb troubles of those early successful years. The brothers were always getting into jams, but they were also always getting out of them. One November weekend in '67, Robin and Molly were returning by train from Hastings where they had visited Molly's family. "Robin had a couple of nights off from the sessions [for **Horizontal**], and we'd gone off to my parents. But Robin wanted to get back." What came next was like something out of one of their songs. Robin: "It was ten o'clock at night, and it's funny because we were just coming into London. We were going about ninety miles an hour, and it was a real built up area, a real city area, and we were talking about wills at the time. All of a sudden, I heard this sort of rattling noise like rocks being thrown to the side of the train, and the lights started flickering inside the cabin. I thought instinctively, 'There's something wrong,' but Molly said that this always happens at this part of the line. I still thought there was something wrong, so I got up to pull the emergency chord. I didn't make it. As I got up, the lights went off and the train went over on its side at ninety miles an hour. There were a lot of people standing in the corridor, and when the train went over on its side, anyone standing in those areas just went." The careering train continued on its destructive path "for about two minutes until it came to a halt. We were upside down, and there was a break

77

in the glass of the door. Imagine if the door had opened. And I looked out and I saw carriages upside down everywhere, over and backwards." Over fifty people were killed and more than one hundred injured in what came to be known as the Hither Green Train Wreck. Miraculously, Robin and Molly only were bruised and frightened. "I got out of the side of the carriage and pulled Molly out. Neither of us was trapped."

It was out of a moment such as this that Robin created one of his most mournful ballads, Molly recalls. "He said, 'I've got this song going on,' He'd bought this beautiful piano-accordion in Paris a few weeks earlier. This song, 'Really and Sincerely,' came about from the mood he was feeling about the train crash." Molly also remembers the birth of one of the group's most popular songs. "We'd had the most dreadful row and weren't talking. Robin will get over an argument very quickly. One minute, he'll have a blazing row, but the next moment, to him, it's forgotten. You're just to carry on as if nothing was said, nothing happened. But with me, I can't. I tend to dwell on it. Anyway, he was being all cheerful again and wanted to talk. I didn't. We'd got a tiny two-room flat, so I was in one room, and he was in the other. He got out a cello and he worked out the beginnings of "I've Just Gotta Get A Message To You' because it was a way of trying to communicate with me. Originally, that song was written with soul singer Percy Sledge in mind."

Barry had been separated from his first wife shortly after the Gibbs arrived in England, and he was enjoying pop stardom as a "bachelor." Dick Ashby: "Barry's line for getting girls into bed was that he would instantly fall in love with them and want to marry them. That's how he would make sure they'd come into bed with him that night. He actually used to carry engagement rings in his pocket on the German tour. So by the end of the tour, I might have six 'fiancees' at the stage door. Horrendous affairs." Ultimately, the woman who became paramount in Barry's life was the one, who in her own words, "never fell for the engagement bit. Whenever he came on about that to me, I'd say, 'Oh, no. I may be Scottish and very naive but I'm not that naive.'"

Linda Gray was a Scottish beauty queen, having been voted Miss Edinburgh in 1967 at the age of 17. Her future with Barry may have been preordained, as she remembers. "When I was 15, me and all my girlfriends in Scotland went to this spiritualist. And she was telling me about lots of different things . . . winning some contest, this and that. I didn't think anything about it. It was rubbish; you just go for a laugh. Then she said, 'I see you with this man. He's got a beautiful head. And he's very musically minded. And he's got a sister Leslie. You don't even know this man. I don't even know if he's in the country [he wasn't]. And there is a blonde woman who will stand in your way.' Barry's first wife was blonde. More or less, that spiritualist told me about Barry."

After winning the beauty contest in the summer of '67, Linda "went to London to be the hostess of 'Top of the Pops.' We were friends with Jimmy Saville, and he always disc-jockeyed the show. I met Barry that day. I didn't know who he was at the time. I was very, very shy and very naive. At rehearsals, I'm with the other girls, and they say, 'This guy keeps looking at you.' I was getting all embarrassed. He came over and introduced himself, and I told him who I was. He looked at me a bit strangely as if to say, 'Oh, she doesn't know who I am.' We went down to the restaurant and had coffee. He invited me to the party they were having later that night at Robert's house in Adam's Row. I said that I'd like to go, but Jimmy wouldn't let me. He was more or less a chaperone for me. He said, 'I'm looking after you for your parents and you're my responsibility.'

"After the show, when we got back to the hotel, I saw this cab waiting there. So I jumped in. Jimmy's assistant jumped in the cab behind me. I said, 'Lose that car,' just like in a movie. They were following me, and I was crying all the way. I don't know why; I just had this strong feeling about Barry. And I was so upset. I thought I was never going to see him again. I got to Adam's Row, and Victor, the manservant who worked for Robert, answered the door. I said, 'I've come to see Barry.' Mascara was running down all over my face, and Victor said, 'I don't know who you are.' Just then, Barry came running down the stairs and said, 'It's OK. I'm expecting her.' We didn't go straight into the patry; we went into the study. Barry was on the phone to his mother, and his wife was threatening to come to the party. I thought, 'My God. He's married. Oh no!' "

When Barry got off the phone, he looked at a very distraught Linda and said, "Don't look so worried. You tell me your problem and I'll tell you mine." "He told me all about his relationship, how he was separated. And then I told him how I shouldn't be there." But Linda stayed. The party that night was to celebrate "Massachusetts" having reached number one. As Linda remembers, "He gave me all the usual crap. 'Oh, I love you' this and that. And I said, 'Oh, yes? How many people have you said that to today?' We saw each other a few times after that when he came to Scotland. When I was eighteen, I came down to do some modeling in London. We met again, and shortly after that, we started living together. I stopped working then because Barry said he didn't want me messing around with photographers. He said, 'You better watch the boys in London.' I thought. 'He's so sweet; he's really nice.' And he was very nice. He was so polite and well-mannered which you don't always find in young guys. He was very romantic, opened the door for me and things like that."

One of the most amusing days in the life of Barry and Linda took place before they were married, and it almost ended their relationship. "After I was living with him," Linda recalls, "the girls used to come to the door. And they were all engaged. One time, Barry was doing this TV thing. I was at home cleaning the flat, so I'm in a scruffy old dress, no make-up. Just how you generally are doing housework. The doorbell rings. It was the penthouse apartment, and the door wouldn't open unless I buzzed the person in. You could look through this eye and see who it was. I saw this chick there and thought, 'Oh!?' because she looked as if she was expected. I opened the door and said, 'Can I help you?' So she says [mimicking the girl's accent], 'Oh yes. I have come to see Barry.' I knew there was some press expected that afternoon so I said, 'Come on in, he won't be long.'

"She made herself very at home, took her coat off and threw it over the chair. She lies back on the chair and says, "Barry and I, we are so in love." Biting her tongue Linda said, "Oh really?" "She says, 'Oh we had such a wonderful time last night at the 'Top of the Pops.' I said, 'Oh you did, did you?' Getting very mad. She said, 'Are you the girl who answers the phone and does things for Barry?' I said, 'Well, you could say that.' She says, 'How long have you worked for Barry?' I said, 'Well, I've just stopped.' She said, 'I do not understand.' I said, 'No? You will.' And she's looking at me very strange.

"I got on the phone to Barry. Keith [Leslie's husband who was working as Barry's personal assistant at the time] answered the phone and said, 'Linda, you sound a bit upset.' 'Who is this girl?' I screamed. 'What are you talking about?' he asks. I say, 'The girl who had such a wonderful time with Barry.' He says, 'Oh no. Are you upset?' I said, screaming, 'Am I upset?' Keith says, 'Don't do anything.' I answered, 'I'm not doing anything, Keith. I'm just going to pack my bags and go.' Then Barry came to the phone. 'Are you all right love?' 'Barry,' I said, 'There's some Swedish girl telling me about you and her last night.' He says, 'Oh, she arrived at 'Top of the Pops' last night. It wasn't my fault. It had happened on a tour before you were around. I said, like I usually said, 'When you come to England, come to see me.' I said, 'I don't believe you'."

Linda continued packing as Keith and Barry rushed home. Linda: "After that incident, Barry started taking me on tour. He said, 'You're coming on tour; then you can't get misled that there's anything going on.' I said OK and unpacked my bags. Barry's divorce was final in the spring of 1970, and he and Linda were married on September 1, 1970. Linda chose that day so that "he would never forget our wedding date 'cause that's his birthday."

Maurice, meanwhile, was building quite a reputation for himself in London's night life scene. "I was loony, with Richard Harris, Michael Caine, Peter O'Toole, Oliver Reed, Alan Bates and Albert Finney. The whole gang of us, the London Mafia, used to go around together drinking a lot." Drinking and cars were Maurice's passions in the late '60s. As Hugh remembers, "Maurice was barely tall enough to drive his Rolls. He used to sit on a phone book so he could see over the hood." "Mo" also had a penchant for getting smashed and driving his expensive cars into the trees that seemed to always be jumping out into the middle of the road. While Maurice does acknowledge that he was pretty crazy in those days, he insists that his reputation for wildness was greatly exaggerated by the press.

Being the most socially inclined of the brothers,

Maurice is always making friends with everybody he meets. In those days, he was also playing the rock star role to the hilt, hitting all the hot spots. One night at the Speakeasy Club was especially memorable. Cream was playing, and the Bee Gees had gone to see their stablemates perform, Cream being the other group signed to Robert Stigwood. "John Lennon was there that night," Maurice recalls, and "he said to us, 'Welcome to the office.' We said, 'Thank you John. Nice to meet you,' and I walked away from him. And he came up to me and said, 'Can I buy you a drink? I don't know what it is, but I like you.' I said, 'Why?' He said, 'Everyone in there wants to lick my boots. You're the first one to tell me to piss off.' I said, 'When I said 'Nice to meet you' and you said 'Naturally,' naturally I thought you were a big-headed bastard.' He said, 'Good for you. Cheers.' And we became friends from then on."

Another star that Maurice met in his social wanderings was Lulu, a pop singer best known in the U.S. for her hit record "To Sir With Love." In England, she has been a big star for years, very much the darling of the press and public. Of course, any romance that she was in was fodder for the gossip sheets that blanket England like the fog. Her romance with Maurice was front page copy, and they were a "hot" item for years. Because the Bee Gees had become big stars in England in such a relative short period of time, there was a great interest in them as people because nobody knew very much about them. The Bee Gees went into the media machine as virtual unknowns, and with his flair for publicity, Robert Stigwood created a very successful record selling unit. But the media game works both ways. Once the Bee Gees were "made" by the press, they then lost all semblance of private lives. Their every action came under public scrutiny. So when Barry took Maurice aside for some brotherly advice, it was more than a little disturbing to pick up the next week's paper and read that Barry had told Maurice not to marry Lulu. As Barry explains, "I never said, 'She's no good for you.' I never said, 'You're no good for her.' I just said, 'You're a little bit young. Why don't you go together for awhile?' I'm the oldest brother, and if I think he's too young to get married, I've got to tell him so. That's all." Barry was only trying to pass along the experience of his first failed youthful marriage, but the hungering press monster grasped the entire episode as more evidence of the dissension that racked the brothers and the Bee Gees. The minor discussions and disagreements were making headlines until they became major problems, and even the brothers began to think they were really feuding. Ultimately, the public backbiting led to the group's break-up.

Although the brothers' wives weren't in any way responsible for the split, the fact that the brothers were no longer living together was all part of the process of growing apart from one another. The closeness that had built towards their success was rapidly disappearing. By late 1968, all that really remained of the Brothers Gibb was the huge success that was the Bee Gees. The Bee Gees were no longer brothers in the loving, caring sense of the word.

Dick Ashby remembers how crazy the times had become "in terms of the boys being able to handle what was happening to them in as much as they became front page newsmakers in England, whatever they did. Barry got caught smuggling some jewelry into the country once; another time, he fired a gun in the air at an intruder. Instead of the intruder getting arrested, Barry did. It was really the fault of the money and their youth and not being able to handle things."

While the Bee Gees have nothing but the highest personal regard for Robert Stigwood and tremendous respect for what he has done for their career, Barry admits that "the fact that we had that amount of money at that age was ludicrous. It should never have been allowed. That's the only criticism I have of Robert. In those days, he should have made sure we had one amount per week and showed us exactly what was in our account that we wouldn't have until a certain time in the future. That way, it would have been protected. We were allowed to have as much as we could spend. I got an award for wearing clothes, a Carnaby St. award, given out based on the fact that I'd spent more money than anybody else on that street in that year. I'd come out of my flat in Eaton Square and every car on the street was my car. I'd say, 'Which one will I drive today, the Rolls or the Lamborghini?' That's ridiculous." As a half-serious aside, Linda points out that "it was only a very small street. There was only room for four or five cars."

The spending, particularly on Barry's part, got way out of hand. Linda remembers watching Barry "go down to the jewelers and he came back with about $10,000 worth of jewelry. I thought, 'I've never seen anybody spend money like this in my life. My God, is he crazy?'" Another time, Linda returned to their apartment to find Barry in the living room, "shooting his BB gun at the chandeliers. They were crazy at times; they did silly things."

It was money and egos and success and publicity that took over the Bee Gees' lives. While Barry went on spending sprees, Maurice got drunk and smashed up cars. Robin "started taking more and more speed. Then I started taking downers. I used to wallow in all those pills." To Barry, "That whole period is just constant speed. I can't remember much what with the dexedrine and all. It was hard to know what time of day it was. We just went from one thing to another. A group that was being promoted in those days never stopped. We must have toured for two straight years. Because of that, the Bee Gees didn't do another tour for years because we were just exhausted."

It was during the making of **Odessa** that the group's problems reached a crisis stage, and the ambitious album project drowned in the Bee Gees sea of difficulties. Barry explains that the original concept was "the story of this man who was ship-wrecked and left floating on an iceberg, and he came from Odessa. He was talking about all his friends, and all these people he knew. The story was supposed to go from there. But it never eventuated. It just got very strange. We didn't know what direction we were going in. We lost track of the story. It was never a finished album. It was our own production, and I think we're proud of that. We put it together. But we were going downhill fast at that point. I don't mean as a group. But Robin's health was—you could not speak to him. There was no communication between him and me and Maurice. It just got way out of hand, blistering arguments. Which was only pills talking, it wasn't us at all. It was just speed and bad temper and nerves. It collapsed underneath us."

Despite everything, **Odessa** was a remarkable achievement. The production was the best the Bee Gees had managed so far and it was considerably more sophisticated than the work of the first three albums. The title track, done mostly by Robin, remains one of the group's most important works. One of the prettiest tunes they've ever written, "Melody Fair," became the title track for a movie, "Melody," and also scored as a number one hit in Japan.

It was the first single from the album, though, that caused the biggest fight yet. "First of May" was released and Robin thought that the flipside, "Lamplight," was going to be the A-side of the disk. He felt snubbed, as if he wasn't getting enough recognition for his artistic contributions. Again, it was "the pills talking."

The swiftness of the Bee Gees' success just proved to be too much. "It was very scary," Maurice explains. "We were so scared. We didn't know what was going on. It caused the break-up." Robin: "We were having the joys of success, but we weren't getting on together. We were still kids and all of a sudden, with success, we had egos and became more sensitive." The rocket ship that had carried the Bee Gees to the top of the music world couldn't survive the strains of fame. In March of 1969, Robin left the Bee Gees, beginning the darkest part of their lives and career. More than anything, Barry blames drugs for the group's problems. "Robin went through the phase of taking uppers and downers. All our sessions, everything we did in 1968 was done taking speed or taking pills. Everyone we met was doing it; it was sort of a cult thing. Everyone was popping pills in the business. It became normal at that point. We never took LSD which is a miracle because the Beatles influenced a lot of people into taking LSD. It's a wonder we didn't do the same thing because we were Beatle-influenced. Everything they did, we thought they were gods. But we just stuck to our purple hearts."

As Maurice admits, "I was the piss artist, Barry the pothead and Robin the pillhead. It was instability. So hard to handle sudden success. Everything was going so fast. One minute, 'Poof!' you've got this; next minute, you can buy that car or this house. Let's do this or that. You get to a stage where it gets out of hand, and you've got to do something to get away from it." Barry: "It was really showing its damage on Robin. Robin suffered a lot. I managed to realize what it was doing, and I stopped. He went into his own world, became a recluse. And we split."

4

BREAK-UP
TO MAKE-UP

1969 and 1970 were the two bleakest years in the Bee Gees' career for the very simple reason that the group didn't really exist from March of '69 until the fall of 1970. And even more painful than the group's split was the fact that the Bee Gees were no longer brothers.

Barry: "We stayed to ourselves, surrounded by hangers-on. Each had his own camp of 'friends' who said he was the real star, he should go solo. When we became isolated, the problems started. We stopped seeing one another as brothers. We were three stars unto ourselves. The pressure and fame got to Robin the most. He's a very deep thinker with a very serious, sensitive side to him. He gets in moods that last quite a while. I remember when things were coming apart in '69, I went over to his house to talk to him, try to straighten things out. All these people were sitting around him. And every time I said something, they'd look at him like, 'Don't listen to him.' This was happening to a family, not just to a rock band. It was terrifying. And I couldn't go as the big brother and tell everyone to calm down. It was impossible with that speed going around."

Robert Stigwood had a five year contract with the Brothers Gibb so he was the target of more than one lawsuit. Robert: "It started when Robin announced that he was leaving the group and going solo. What tends to happen, of course, when a new group breaks and becomes very big, all sorts of hangers-on get around them. So each brother had his set of advisors who would tell them they should be doing this, that and the other thing. They [Barry and Maurice] were so upset by Robin's departure that we had to release Robin from the company. That was really the most difficult part of it. I always instinctively knew that they'd get back together—there's a great bond there for them as brothers. But when brothers fight, it's really worse than strangers fighting." Robin was suing for his freedom, and he and Barry exchanged rather heated words in the press. As Maurice recalls, "I was in the middle. It was always Barry saying this about Robin one week in the music trades, and Robin answering him back and vice versa. And I'm going, 'Will somebody please ask me what's going on.' I was always in the middle, so I never got involved in the argument."

All of the ego-clashing and success had divided the family and it would take quite a lot to put all the pieces together again. The events surrounding the split, as reported dutifully and gleefully by the press, were quite distasteful. The worst of all was when Hugh went to court to try and have Robin declared a ward of the court. Hugh explains that "certain people around him were trying to rip him off, but he wouldn't listen. I could see what was happening. They were trying to make Robin a big star. I wanted him made a ward of the court for his own protection. It was the only way I could see it so these people couldn't get at him. That was the only answer at that time."

Robin and Molly had only been married a few months when the split happened, and she was in a very difficult position. Looking back with the vantage of almost a decade's perspective, it is still painful for Molly to discuss those times. What Molly expresses most of all is her devotion to Robin. "I think the whole thing was blown up out of all proportion. Robin has got a mind of his own, always has. He wanted to leave the group, and as his wife, I was behind him. If your husband wants to do something, you're not going to kick him in the teeth. He wanted to do it, so I stood by him, no matter what. I don't know why his family and people surrounding him thought he wasn't capable of making his own decisions. That's when the nervous exhaustion bit [from the early tour] came back and was thrown in our faces. To make your son a ward of the court when he's a married man, to me, was just absolutely crazy. And I took it because I'm that kind of person. It was terribly unpleasant, and it was very upsetting for my family. We're just an ordinary family, and to pick up the papers and read this and that. And, of course, we had no money. Our money was stopped. The whole thing was like a crazy nightmare. All Robin wanted was to have more recognition of himself as a songwriter and a singer, not as a personality."

Barry was a most interested and distressed observer to the entire time, but he puts it in an objective light. "Both Dad and Mom didn't have evil in them. They didn't have anything against Molly. They were only trying to save Robin from what he was doing to himself and that was speeding. They tried to stop it to get him in his right mind. They thought somebody was doing everything for him. Robin wasn't doing anything. He was vegetating. He didn't know one way or the other what he wanted to do. That's the way I saw it. And, of course, it alienated Molly from our parents." With great despair in his voice, Barry adds, "For forever, I suppose." In publicly discussing this part of their lives for the first time, the Gibb family acknowledges the existence of hurt feelings. It is also clear that the cliche, 'time heals all wounds,' appears to be working. Barry expresses the hope that "they both see reason in the end and get back together and discuss what happened. Unless it's discussed between Mom, Dad, and

Molly, it'll never really become a total calm. It'll always exist somewhere in the back of their minds."

One of the more unusual events in Bee Gees history came next. With sister Leslie taking Robin's place, the Bee Gees did a TV special, "Talk of the Town." That was the first and only time Leslie has sung publicly with her brothers, and she felt that it "seemed to go well, though I was very nervous. I nearly burst into tears when it all began." As Barbara recalls, Leslie told her after the show that she was "praying. She said, 'It was like a movie, being on that stage, hoping that all at once, Robin would just walk on stage.' She said, 'That would have really been the end, if he had just walked on.' And Robin was feeling that himself. Of course, it never happened, but it would have been great." Leslie never performed again as a Bee Gee, although she did give momentary consideration to a singing career. At the last minute, Leslie decided to return to Australia with her husband and leave show business behind.

She left Barry, Maurice and Colin to continue the Bee Gees. That line-up didn't survive the making of the first Bee Gees movie. "Cucumber Castle," named after a song from **Bee Gees 1st,** "should have been amazing," Barry recalls. "It was terrible. It was an hour TV special. The script was changed by a very silly TV director. Nobody had any good lines. I'd written a script with Robin that was, to me, hysterical, the whole thing. And they didn't want to use it because it wasn't slapstick. So we ended up hitting each other with pies." Maurice remembers that "it was good fun to do basically because of the people that were in it . . . Vincent Price, Spike Milligan and Frankie Howerd who played our father in it. We had a lot of fun, more fun making it than I think it turned out."

During the making of "Cucumber Castle," the brothers and Colin had a falling out. Maurice explains: "Colin said he didn't want to be in any of the sketches or the skits. He just wanted to be in the musical numbers. So we said 'OK, if that's what you want.' The next minute, we got a letter from his lawyers saying that he hasn't got enough to do in the film. So Robert said, 'OK, he's fired.' ' In one of the most absurd episodes of the Bee Gees' career, Colin sued Barry and Maurice, claiming that they didn't have the right to continue to work as a pop group using the name the Bee Gees. A bemused judge threw the case out of court, and the Bee Gees were two.

The two-thirds Bee Gees recorded an album of songs for "Cucumber Castle." Meanwhile, Robin released his first solo single, "Saved by the Bell." It soared to number two in the British charts. But, as Maurice notes, "we were originally recording that for the new album. Barry couldn't make the session, so we put it down. Robin and I did it. Then he split, and later released it as a single." In discussing those times, Robin sums it all up with a simple statement. "I don't know what I was thinking at the time, because I was so screwed up." The Bee Gees first single from **Cucumber Castle**, "Don't Forget to Remember," followed Robin's record up the charts to number one, but those were the last significant hits the Gibbs would have for more than a year.

In the fall of 1969, studio time was booked for a new "Gee Bees" album which Robert Stigwood suggested the group make even though neither Barry nor Maurice really wanted to record. The first day of the sessions, Barry remembers that he "got on IBC studios. Maurice knows well and truly about it. And there's nobody there! So I called up Robert, and said, 'Where's Maurice? We're supposed to be doing an album.' Robert said, 'He's in Australia.' I said, 'Robert, you've lined all this up for us to go in the studio and make an album. Why didn't Maurice even tell me he was going to Australia?' And he said, 'Well, he went with Lulu

The day in August of 1958 when the Gibb family left England for Australia. A pensive Barry stands between his parents, twins Robin and Maurice wait patiently at right, baby Andy rides in his mother's arms and sister Leslie holds cousin Mark.

On their wedding day in 1944, Hugh and Barbara stroll beneath an arch of instruments formed by Hugh's band.

The twins Maurice and Robin.

Barry leads brothers Robin (left) and Maurice and chums in song, circa 1956.

YES, THEY'RE REAL COOL CATS

THREE boys from Redcliffe who have jolted the radio and record world with a "rockabilly" song . . . Barry Gibb (left) and his 9-year-old twin brothers, Maurice and Robin. The song they're singing is their own.

Three boys 'rock' the song world

A newspaper feature, dated 1960. The "rockabilly song" was Barry's own composition, "Let Me Love You."

The Bee Gees were growing out of their "clubland" image in Australia.

Collectively catching arthritis.

1960: Appearing as regulars on Australian TV "Bandstand," similar to "American Bandstand" in the U.S.

After the cyclone hit.

Under Robert Stigwood's guidance, the Bee Gees prepare for their 1968 extravaganza appearance at London's Royal Albert Hall. The group was backed by a 67-piece orchestra, a 50-piece Royal Air Force band and a huge choir.

"The winkle pickers in Australia." Circa 1964. "You couldn't get Beatles boots or Mersey boots. Only Italian pointed toes." Note: Maurice could not stand properly on his.

1968: One man and his Rolls. Maurice converts his first major earnings into wheels.

A 1967 appearance on England's "The Simon Dee Show." The Bee Gees call it, "Our insane attempt to create a trend in clothes. Instead, we were knocked for looking like baboons."

Robin and Molly wed, December 4, 1968

Twelve-year-old Andy wonders what all the fuss is about as he tries to help his brothers carry the bride for photographers.

...uary 1969, Maurice and Lulu honeymoon in Acapulco with ...y and Linda along as "advisors."

1970: Together again! One of the first formal portraits after the historic reconciliation.

1968: In full makeup for the British TV special, "Frankie Howerd Meets The Bee Gees."

1969: Sister Leslie's one and only TV appearance, standing in for Robin on the British "The Talk Of The Town" show.

October 17, 1975, Maurice and Yvonne wed.

Robin and Molly at home with Melissa and Spencer who was named for Robin's hero, Winston Spencer Churchill.

Maurice and Yvonne with Adam.

Linda with Ashley; Barry with Steven.

On seeing Mum and Dad both naked for the first time.

1978: The platinum car given to Maurice, Robin and Barry by
Robert Stigwood.

Andy Gibb: "They have been my biggest influence and my biggest help. There's a magic when we work together . . . Imagine having the greatest singers and songwriters living under one roof. Your roof . . . Their harmonies, the ballads, all influenced me greatly . . . I guess you could say I idolized the Bee Gees as a band, and loved them as brothers."

Robin's fantasy.

Barry's fantasy.

Maurice's fantasy.

1976: Key to New York City. Barry, Robin and Maurice honored by then N.Y. Mayor Abraham Beame for contributing concert proceeds to the Police Athletic League.

quickly. It had to be done quickly. They've gone to promote 'Cucumber Castle.' I said, 'What!?' Things were pretty crazy, but nothing as crazy as this. I honestly felt at the time that I was being worked against. So I never really left the group. The group left me in a way." By the end of 1969, all that was left of the Bee Gees was a mountain of actual and threatened legal action.

Andy Gibb, who since 1976 has emerged as a solo singing star, was barely a teenager when his older brothers split up, but he still remembers the pain. "It was a very shaky thing as far as our family went, because it was a sore point. My brothers weren't talking to each other, and they all wanted to because they're so close. They can't get by a week without talking to each other, and they wanted to call but no one wanted to swallow their pride and do it. The family was going through a real tight moment 'cause it affected my parents and everything. For families to split up, it's really a strange thing. I knew they were going to get back together again, and our family knew. There was no doubt about that, but it was hard for the public to know that."

It was a depressing time for the brothers, and it had to negatively affect their creative output. Neither Barry's nor Maurice's solo singles are memorable, and Robin's solo LP, **Robin's Reign,** is one record that Robin would rather forget. "To me, it's unfinished. You've got to realize how many ideas I had. The reason I didn't finish it was because I had so many legal problems at that time to take care of as a leftover from the Bee Gees. So did everyone else. Until that was sorted out, I couldn't really concentrate on recording." Both Maurice and Barry recorded solo albums during the split, but the tapes remained "in the can" when the group got back together. During that time, Maurice also appeared on the London stage in a musical, "Sing a Rude Song." "It was an experience, and I'll never do it again as long as I live. I hated it . . . dancing around like a half-assed clown."

In 1970, Robert Stigwood was involved in turning RSO into a public corporation, and this created more problems for the Gibb brothers. As major shareholders in RSO, the Bee Gees found themselves the targets of unnamed financiers who wanted to gain control of RSO. Barry recalls that when "the financial battle was going on, none of us were left alone night and day. Other people, other major people, other important people were trying to buy our shares. They were harassing us and persecuting us. All kinds of death threats, threats to our families, things like that. 'Sell your shares [or else]'."

According to Barry, "we always seemed to have enough money so that during the time the pressure was on, we were all right. Providing we didn't give way to those people who threatened physical violence. They didn't actually commit physical violence, but sent heavies to our door, just to bang on the door. Not to get in, not to do anything but frighten the lives out of us. I can't say who sent them . . . various major concerns." Robert Ştigwood remembers that Robin was getting pressured because Robin "had the crucial one per cent controlling share, and he was threatened by some heavies to give it up." As Molly recalls, "I think it hit us hardest because there were times when there was no money at all around, and Robin wasn't working, it was like, 'What are we going to pawn this week?' "

Barry points to the entire troubled time as an invaluable "part of the maturing. I realized that the business wasn't all stars and flowers, which it was at that time . . . peace and love. It sure wasn't all that. It makes you a bit hard, more steely. You don't become so easily played with as you might have been under different circumstances. We grew up fast at that point." Linda notes that the brothers, "especially Barry, did a lot of spending when they didn't actually have it in liquid cash. It was advances and loans, and one day, the office goes public and they say, 'Well, you have this debt with us.' and all of a sudden, you're asked to pay it. I think that brought them all back down to earth."

In their minds, the brothers were already beginning to wonder what caused the split, and it was this awakening that was the first seeds of a reunion. Robin recalls being "in my house watching television one day feeling somewhat pissed off, 'cause I knew what we were doing or what we were trying to do separately was what we could all do together. Barry was in Spain, and I rang him there and said, 'Let's get back together and go into the studios.' He said we'd have to talk about it when he got back to London. It wasn't all as easy as that. It was six months later when we finally got around to getting into the studio." Being a solo artist, as Robin explains, just wasn't any fun. "When you're doing something on your own and have success, you can't really share it with anyone. We were so used to sharing our success. When you are successful on your own, you turn around and say, 'Hey, how about this?' and there's no one there. I was going through court cases and everything like that with accountants and other people. Everybody was suing each other. I didn't know what it was all about. Everybody had miserable faces, and there I was sitting with a number two record. So I decided that wasn't much fun at all."

"It was pretty nasty in the boardroom," Dick Ashby recalls, "but it wasn't really the boys so much. Robin had gone off and was doing a deal with NEMS enterprise. So NEMS lawyers and RSO lawyers were having pretty hefty meetings on Robin's behalf, splitting his wares, as it were. Barry was unavailable in his apartment in London. But as far as the three brothers were concerned, it wasn't heavy because they weren't seeing each other. There was some obviously hairy business going on, but at the time, the boys weren't too business-minded. So it was more or less left to lawyers. History has shown it was whether they had a good or bad lawyer in those days as to how they'd come out of it, with what slice of the pie they got." It was eventually business that got the brothers together. Dick Ashby: "At the time, RSO was going public, and with their assets in the company, they were very much involved financially. Robert had to get them in one at a time to sign papers, discuss their new share deal and their new parts in the company. I think, once again, Stiggy's got to be credited with it. He said to them, 'Look, we're going public . . . What a great thing it would be to launch the public company presswise if you all came back together."

"After a period of time, when tempers had cooled, I made them all have a meeting." Manager Robert Stigwood describes the split and how he brought the group back together. "There was a period when the brothers weren't speaking to one another and I think they all got a little older and a little wiser. It was very difficult. Don't forget that in those days, Robin and Maurice were teenagers. To be a hit with all that success at such a young age is very difficult to contend with. I think they really needed time, and it did them a lot of good in many ways to have the separation and then come back together again." The actual reunion, according to Robert, "came from themselves wanting to do it, and also at the same time, I was taking the company public in England and it was very important for them to participate in that, so that added the business impetus."

Remembering the business considerations, Barry claims "that was all a game. Spiritually, our heads weren't in it. We were still upset with each other.

Things hadn't been resolved. And Robert was putting us back together in his way, meaning well, of course. But really to the ends of seeing the company going on the market united. Everything we did was for the corporation. I honestly think the will was there for us to come back together. I don't think the time was right for us. It was all done legally. Everybody had their lawyer in the room, and nothing was resolved. Robin's problem was still there. At that point, there was a battle going on over who could get the most amount of shares before the company went pulbic." Other than Polygram/Polydor, which was the major financier of RSO, "I think Robert and David (Shaw) had the most. Then me, Maurice and Robin and Eric Clapton, Jack Bruce, Ginger Baker and Frankie Howard, down the line. What was going on was a major corporate battle. The Bee Gees couldn't survive during that. No one was looking after the Bee Gees. It was a total financial struggle. Except you couldn't have put that in magazines. Nobody would have listened to you."

Regardless of the motivations for the reunion, "I think the most important time that affected me most," Maurice reflects, "was when the three of us were sitting in the office in London. We'd split up, and the lawyers and the accountants were all there, trying to sort out all our affairs with Robert. We all looked at each other like, 'What the bloody hell are we doing here?' All these people are trying to fight over who owns what, and who gets this and that, and our manager is sitting there trying to sort them all out. We're sitting there together on the couch going, 'What's going on?' We wanted to get back together again. And all of a sudden, the four of us, Robert as well, realized these guys were trying to break us up, not keep us together. And when we got around to Barry's part, I broke up and cried 'cause I couldn't believe how stupid we'd been. My first wife [Lulu] just sat there going, 'Take it easy.' I said, 'I just don't believe the rubbish we're going through. We have so much for each other, and we're separating it." Robin: "There were all these people giving us this 'Don't speak to anybody until you speak to me' business. We got back together because we wanted to." Robin's solo album had already been released, as Maurice remembers, but "Barry and I went, 'Let's leave our solo albums out. We decided not to promote his album or release ours. We decided to go back into the studio, and we recorded the **Two Years On** album," the title a direct reference to the length of the split between the brothers.

Once the decision to again become the Bee Gees had been made, it was up to the brothers to go into the studio and try and recapture their magic. While they had immediate success as recordmakers, Maurice claims "it took us a good four years to get back to the original group." Barry: "We knew it would take us five years to get to know each other again as brothers. We certainly weren't brothers at that point. We discussed it at great length because we know we care about each other. We're now back to where we were before we ever made it . . . back to reality, with our feet on the ground."

Remarkably, the first song they recorded, "Lonely Days," became their biggest hit ever in America, reaching number three in Billboard and number one in Cashbox, their first chart-topper in the U.S. Their second single, "How Can You Mend A Broken Heart," did even better, becoming an across-the-board number one. Within a year of getting back together, the Bee Gees were again making hits. However, something was missing, because the Bee Gees' success faded as quickly as it happened and 1972–1974 were years filled with unsuccessful records. Personal success, too, wasn't easily achieved.

Robin explains that "we all had a hunk of pride to

swallow. What had happened was really nothing at all. We were all reading press articles about what critics were saying about us, and we were just going on that and not how each other really felt. I think after we started working together again, we realized that it was just what the press made of it, and not what we had made of it." Still, there are scars, Robin: "It was murder, the biggest nightmare that I've ever gone through, and it has been for the three of us. The press just made our lives hell, and they made it so bad for us . . . those days left a sort of mark on me. I could never understand why people wrote and said the things they did about us when all we did was break up." Robert Stigwood points out that "the English public didn't take kindly to the break-up because of the press. They really had a field day with it. So there were lots of unpleasant quotes from one brother about the other one. That didn't win any sympathy from anyone. Because from public's point of view, they were sort of riding high, earning a lot of money. And then to see that go on, we decided the best thing was to focus on their recording and not worry about the publicity."

Those earliest reunion recording sessions, according to Robin, were "just a nerve thing. There were barriers between us, and we had to break down those barriers." Maurice notes that "when we got back together, I was married. I had my house and one car, and that was it. I was stable. I'd grown up. Barry, especially, made me grow up very quickly because I was watching him and I went, 'That's right.' And I came up with things to him and he goes, 'Christ. You've grown up, haven't you?' All of a sudden, the three of us came to the same level." Molly speaks for everyone when she says that if the break-up "hadn't have happened then, they wouldn't be together now. I'm convinced of that. The time away gave them all breathing space, time to grow up. And to realize that as a team they worked better.

Everything had been so intense. They'd almost been manipulated like puppets. And they were very much indulged in. I think this type of break made them realize what it was all about."

In 1971, the publicity happy Bee Gees embarked on an extensive tour that would take them to America, and back to Australia for the first time since they'd left in 1967. However, there were still bad times ahead for the brothers. Barry: "Robin was still doing the speed, still on the way down. We arrived in Greensboro, North Carolina, one night. The next morning, I walked past Robin's room, and the door was slightly open. My father was standing in the middle of the room, and Robin was laying out on the middle of the bed. He'd collapsed. The stress of the overwork combined with the pills was too much for him. Really, all he needed was to rest and get his head clear."

The Bee Gees cancelled their concert appearance for the evening, the first show in their whole lives they'd ever missed, but it was a small price to pay for Robin's well-being. As Barry recalls, Robin spent a few days in the hospital taking it easy and "within five days, Robin was wrestling with the doctors, stuffing himself with hamburgers and demanding to be let out. Five or six days later, he appeared onstage with us again. He was a very weak person, and he could hardly sing a note. But the fact was that he was out onstage! The audience knew something had been terribly wrong because the night before, we worked without him. We'd announced that he'd had to go in the hospital, but they didn't know why. A lot of people who came that night also came the next. So they knew that Robin hadn't appeared. When they saw him onstage, they stood up, gave him a standing ovation. Molly flew over from England when she heard all about it, and she was with him [on tour] from then onwards. He started putting on weight slowly, and he's mellowed out over the years, and now he's fine. He's become a normal human being again." This chapter in the Bee Gees story is crucial to understanding the group's perseverance in remaining together for more than two decades. The Bee Gees struggle was much more than a fight for hit records. It was a personal battle that was only won because of the deep family love.

The early '70s weren't just a time when the Bee Gees had a few hits records and then dropped out of the mass public consciousness. The years from 1971–1974 were years of growth and maturation and recovery and transition. The international success that had struck the Gibb family like a thunderbolt had totally disrupted their lives as individuals and as a family unit as well. Each brother had his own struggle growing up. Barry, being the oldest when success hit, had it the easiest. His life was basically the most stable. Maurice and Robin were still teenagers when they became millionaires. Each found it difficult to cope. Robin took his refuge in pills and Maurice in drink. Robin's story is the most dramatic of the three because he hurt himself the worst, but in many respects, all of the brother's personal troubles were necessary. By learning how to handle their lives as "pop stars," the Gibbs were preparing themselves for their next bout with big success.

In the group's first successful era, the Bee Gees' songs tended to be about characters. The Bee Gees would write and sing the songs through the character's eyes. Because of that, a certain observer's detachment appeared in their vocals. After the reunion, the lyrical slant shifted inward. Barry feels that this change was a major factor in the group's inability to sustain the quick success of two huge singles in a row. "I think the biggest mistake you can make in making records is to write about yourself. People are not interested in you just writing about you. They also want to hear your fantasy story. As soon as we stopped writing about ourselves and started writing outward, everyone wanted to know. When we started writing about 'Nights On Broadway,' about a girl who became a star, anybody but ourselves. If you can assume the identity of somebody else, to write a song, you're in much better shape than just writing about your own experience." In between "Run To Me," a moderate hit in the summer of 1972, and "Jive Talkin' " and "Nights On Broadway" in 1975, the Bee Gees were virtually hitless.

"We didn't know where we were going," Barry remembers. "That's why it took so long to break through. We ended up doing dreary ballads, and that was totally wrong. Had a ballad hit with ". . . Broken Heart" and from that moment on, Atlantic didn't want anything else but ballads. We seemed to be stuck in that mode." Even in that mode, the Bee Gees crafted a number of interesting albums and each one contained at least one standout cut like "Saw A New Morning" from **Life In a Tin Can.** Another one of the best songs from that era was the title song on **Trafalgar.** To Maurice, that record was a turning point. "Barry began to respect me for my bass playing, my musical ability. The **Trafalgar** album started that because I wrote the theme, 'Trafalgar,' and recorded it all by myself. And then I just played it for him, and went, 'What do you think?' And he said, 'You don't have to touch it. It's mixed, mastered, finished.' I felt like 'Good grief, he likes my music,' That's how I got more involved in songwriting. Now it's just completely mutual." Having been overshadowed by his brothers in the late '60s, Maurice was rapidly maturing as a writer and producer in the early '70s. One of his solo production efforts, for the group Tin Tin, "Toast and Marmalade For Tea." was a big hit in America. 'Tin Tin' included a young man by the name of Steve Kipner.

The Bee Gees had remembered another friend from their Australian days.

"I call those days the quiet days for the Bee Gees because it was our transition period," notes Robin, "We didn't expect immense success because we were going over. We were getting out of the old Bee Gees, wanted the old Bee Gees to go away. We wanted people to just forget about the old Bee Gees. That is the only way we could not suffocate. We had a couple of transitional albums which we weren't really happy with in this '72-'74 period." The group just wasn't connecting with either the public or their own musical roots. For these three ambitious and forward looking artists, it was a terribly frustrating time. Tom Kennedy has worked as the Bee Gees road manager for nearly a decade (when he replaced Dick Ashby who became the group's personal manager), and Tom remembers those down times. "They knew they were in the doldrums, but they didn't want it aired about them. The close immediate circle of people could say it, and they wouldn't mind. But they wouldn't like someone to walk up and say, 'Oh, it must be awful for you now being so big then and struggling now.' That would upset them." Barry seconds that thought. "Those years were hell. There is nothing worse than being in the pop wilderness. It's like being in exile. And the other artists treat you like crap. They say, 'Hey, I didn't know you were still together.' It's then you realize they haven't thought of you for years. It's all ego. This whole business is ego."

If any one event in those days personified the group's problems, it was a series of shows they gave in early 1974 at the Batley Variety Club in the north of England playing their greatest hits to an inattentive crowd. As Molly recalls, "they were at a really low point in their careers. And it was getting to be, 'what are we gonna do?' There was no way they would have

103

fallen into a trap of doing one-night stands again, and sort of becoming a nothing group and struggling on. Robin's a positive thinker and will not be defeated. If a record doesn't go, it's not going to bring him down. He will be more determined that the next one is going to go. Anyway, Dick Ashby suggested, 'Why don't we do one or two club dates?' Robin had always hated night-clubs because of Australia. They didn't like to go into a night club and see beer-swigging men talking and ignoring what you're doing. Robin wasn't very keen on the idea, but there was nothing much else happening. It was quite a lucrative fee, and it was ready cash.

"After they signed the contract, Robin knew that it was a mistake and he didn't want to do it. He would have done anything not to have done it. Anyway, they went ahead and did it. He really hated every minute of that." Robin: "We thought, 'we've come to this,' and we just walked out of that club and we never looked back. We said 'That is never ever going to happen to this group.' We knew we've got so much to offer." Barry feels that "we'd lost the will to write great songs. We had the talent, but the inspiration was gone." Molly: "Robin said, 'Nothing has changed about performing in front of nightclub audiences.' He came back from that very down. He said, 'It can't be like this. It's not going to be like this. Something has got to happen. I'd rather give up than do that again.' It's like a nightmare to him."

Tom Kennedy thinks that as depressing as those shows were, "it was a good thing in one way because it showed them what not really trying could do and where you could end up. If you try and do something and it doesn't happen, you think maybe it's finished. And I think maybe they were beginning to accept that when Batley came around. That was so bad for them, young people eating while they were performing. They thought, "How can anyone do this?' From that point on, they went for broke. And they made an album that was worthy of being called a Bee Gees album," **Mr. Natural.**

While the group left Batley, with a depressing lesson learned and new resolve to try harder, Maurice left having met his future wife. Yvonne Spencely was the manager of the steak restaurant that was attached to Batley and met Maurice on the second night of the Bee Gees week at Batley. Maurice "had been separated about a month, and it was all over the papers, Lulu being their darling. I was the mean miserable old bastard who treated her like shit, you know? And belted her about now and again. Believe you me, she had a great right hook. Anyway, Derek Smith, the booking agent for Batley, came backstage after the Tuesday show. And he brought Yvonne in to say hello. And she just smiled. And I thought, 'What a beautiful smile!' " Yvonne remembers that "on Friday night, he asked me to live with him. I wouldn't go straight away. I went out with him for a few months. He seemed really nice, a very warm person. That's what struck me first of all. The first night, all I remember was he just kept looking at me and chatting away. Of course, I was more quiet then. All I did was smile."

With the problems within the Bee Gees and in his marriage to Lulu, Maurice had been a troubled man. Those who knew him in those days speak in awe of the changes Maurice underwent once he met Yvonne. Maurice calls it "love at first sight. I couldn't believe that smile, that sort of shimmer in her eyes, laughing teary eyes. When she smiles, you don't know whether she's laughing or crying. That smile really knocked me out. I thought, 'What a lovely girl.' There was a pure innocence about her which is what I loved. She was something that I never thought I'd come across. I was quite thrilled. Changed my life as quickly as that." Yvonne and Maurice were married on October 17,

1975. If ever there was a perfect example of "opposites attracting," Yvonne and Maurice are that couple. Where Maurice is the most extroverted of the Gibb Brothers, Yvonne is the quietest Bee Gee wife. Partly, that's because she's a comparative newcomer to the family, and partly it's because she is very simply a sweet, shy woman. Yvonne is now one of the family, and she and Maurice are very happy. According to Yvonne, Maurice sees to that. "Sometimes, I'll get up in the morning and I'm not always in a good mood. I'll say to Maurice, 'How can you get up in the morning smiling and joking?' And he says, 'Sometimes, I don't feel in a good mood, but it's nice to give out to everyone else, for them to be in a good mood, too.' "

The Brothers Gibb may have only enjoyed a few hit records in the early '70s, but of greater personal consequence was that they became fathers. Robin and Molly were first with a son, Spencer, born September 21, 1972. On December 1, 1973, Linda gave birth to Barry's first son, Stephen. Spencer soon had a sister with the arrival of Melissa of June 17, 1974. Tom Kennedy: "We were in the Record Plant in Hollywood, and the news came through. Robin was at home and when we came in, he was asleep on the floor. He'd been waiting up just to tell us about Spencer. He woke up, and he was really excited. The night Barry's first son was born, he was up all night ringing people." Barry and Linda's second son, Ashley, was born on September 7, 1977. Barry was there for both births.

Maurice and Yvonne have only one child so far, but Maurice worked a lot harder. Adam was born on February 23, 1976, and Maurice was right in the delivery room to help. Yvonne remembers, "He was there for the birth. He was great. He'd been working during the back of my pregnancy. They were away two and a half months, and I'm getting bigger and bigger. I didn't really mind because he used to phone me every night.

106

He came home about three days before I was to go in the hospital. When I went into labor, he came in with gloves on. And he cut the cord. And the doctor said to me, 'Congratulations, you've got a son.' And Maurice came over to me and said, 'It's a boy'." To Maurice, the birth of his son is the highlight of his life. "I got him as he came out, and the doctor grabbed him with me as well. And he said, 'You cut there,' and I cut the cord. They gave him to a nurse, and we washed him down. Then I saw it was a boy."

During the first half of the 1970s, the Bee Gees spent a lot of time touring, trying to recapture some of the old fans and create new ones. And they were very successful. With extensive and frequent tours of the U.S., Canada, Australia and the Far East, the Bee Gees may not have always played to overflow crowds but they always sang to enthusiastic fan response and critical praise for the precision and professionalism of their live performances. Hugh recalls "one of the nicest thing said about them. A reviewer wrote, 'They came onstage looking like every photo of them ever taken and sounding like every record they'd ever made.' "

The Gibb family was on the road a lot in the '70s, too. Different parts of the family lived in Ibiza, Spain, for a while until the repression of Franco became too much. It was in Ibiza that Andy first began to sing. He would often appear in a local club with just a guitar, but it wasn't an unusual sight for both Maurice and Barry to jam with Andy, who was still a few years from stardom. After Ibiza, the Gibbs moved back to the Isle of Man, most for tax reasons. Only Robin accepted the huge bite of the English government, and he and Molly have lived on a beautiful estate in Surrey for the better part of a decade.

One of the more overlooked aspects of the Bee Gees recent rise to superstar status has been the fine band that they work with. Maurice notes that "when we first got back together, we were still wary of each other in the studio, who would sing what, or cause another argument for no reason. It ended up that none of us did any of that at all. All we were worried about was, 'Have we got a good band?' Now we can say that we've got a damn good band together." Slowly, they assembled a fine cast of players. Geoff Bridgeford was the first new member, joining as drummer. Geoff had played with Tin Tin as well as Australia's Steve and The Board. He was also the last non-Gibb to become a Bee Gee. When he departed after a couple of years, the Bee Gees became solely the three Brothers Gibb.

The longest lasting member of the Bee Gees band is lead guitarist Alan Kendall, who had once been part of an English band called Toefat. He joined in 1970. Next, Dennis Bryon replaced Bridgeford on drums, and he's been there ever since. Dennis also brought along an old mate, keyboard man "Blue" Weaver. Dennis and Blue had played together in two English groups, Brother John & the Witnesses and Amen Corner. The latter was a very successful band in the U.K., although they never enjoyed international success. Before hooking up with the Bee Gees, Blue had also been a member of two fine British rock outfits, the Strawbs and Mott the Hoople. These three men have been with the group at least four years each, and it has been with that time and commitment to each other that the Bee Gees have evolved into a band in both a musical and personal sense.

One element of the Bee Gees live sound that was a hallmark of this era was the presence of an orchestra. First Bill Shepherd and then Geoff Westley were the musical directors for the group on the road. As the Bee Gees traveled from town to town, the musical director would assemble the finest string players in each city and rehearse with them the afternoon before a concert. So when the Bee Gees took the stage at night, their sensitive ballads were complemented and cloaked in the stirring sound of strings. As keyboard string synthesizers developed during the '70s, the Bee Gees added them to the live mix until by 1976, the Bee Gees found that as a live performing band, they were better without an orchestra. Of course, the strings are irreplaceable, but as Robin notes, "For years, people said that because we always worked with an orchestra, they never knew if we were any good as a band. It was time to let everybody hear us as a band, so they could judge for themselves." As the Bee Gees music has grown funkier with more R & B material, the synthesizers are the perfect sound.

The first half of this decade may not have been a time for huge international success for the Bee Gees, but it was more than isolated pockets of fans that kept them going. The European continent and England were not "hot spots" for the group, but they could tour the U.S. regularly and know that a fanatical following would be there. And as Tom Kennedy points out, "They enjoy performing. They're performers no matter how big or small the crowd, If it's 60,000 or 3,000, they do as good a show. With that energy coming from the audience, they're enjoying themselves, and the show is going to be as good night after night." That standard of performing excellence would prove invaluable throughout those "down" years because the Bee Gees visited many unusual places.

Dick Ashby remembers that "the weirdest one of all was Jakarta in Indonesia. We did a tour of Australia and the promoter in London who'd bought the whole tour asked if we'd like to do a few gigs in the Far East on the way home. I though it would break up the flight, and they seemed quite excited about visiting Indonesia, Hong Kong, and all these places. The only details I had about this particular Indonesian venue was that it was called Senegahn Stadium, that it was under cover and had 10,000 seats, so we set the fee accordingly. When we got to Jakarta, we went to look at the venue before the band came down, to get the stage and everything together. The taxi driver took us to a most enormous place, the size of Wembley Stadium [an English football arena that holds nearly 100,000]. So I said, 'Oh no, this can't be right,' but sure enough, there was a stage there. It turned out that somehow the venue had been switched on us. There was a lot of tension through the day with me trying to get the fee up, and equipment and staging is very difficult out there, so we had a very hard day at the gig. Then, about an hour before the show was due to start, there was a torrential downpour of rain so all the equipment had to be bunged under the stage—total disaster.

"By this time, all the people were coming, including the Prime Minister of Indonesia who was in the royal box. Tom came to me and said, 'Look, I'm scared of the group going on; it's wet, a guitar's only got to touch something and someone will get electrocuted.' So I went back to the hotel with this in mind, and told the promoter we weren't going on. The promoter's wife burst into tears, saying you must go on, the royal family is there. So in the end, the promoter says to me, 'If the support group goes on and they don't get killed, will you go on?' What could I say to that? I think when the concert started, we had three live mikes. Every time Maurice moved from his stand-up mike to the piano, someone had to go on stage and take his vocal mike across to him. It was an amazingly good sound, and it was quite a good show."

On that same tour, Ashby recalls "two other Indonesian dates, Surabaya and Medan. I don't think there were any cars in the town, people were being pulled around in rickshaws and stuff like this. Tom and I went down to the venue in the afternoon and it was a market. People were buying vegetables and the like.

And this is where we were playing. So I sent Tom back to the hotel and said, 'Tell everybody not to come down until tonight.' By the time night fell, the vegetables were gone and the lights were dimmed, and it didn't look too bad when the band arrived. Until it started raining. And they were playing under a tin roof canopy. The noise from the roof was awful. Probably the worst we ever played."

In the Far East, the Bee Gees had never stopped having hits. "Melody Fair," from Odessa was a big hit, and singles such as "My World" and "Wouldn't I Be Someone" were number one in places like Hong Kong. For some reason, possibly the language barrier, the Bee Gees seemed to do the oddest things in Japan. Linda recalls how some members of the touring party kept things interesting. "Dennis [Bryon], Barry and I all decided we were going to do something silly because it was the last night of the tour." The afternoon before the show, the three conspirators got big bags of rice and flour. They then took paper towels, put rice in the bottom of each one to weigh it down, put in a handful of flour and tied the towel up with an elastic band. Hundreds of flour bombs were made, and when Alan Kendall uncovered the plot he made his own stack. Linda: "Everyone had these piles of flour bombs."

On that tour, Linda remembers, "Robin was always dressed in black." During a concert, he perspired freely, so he kept a towel by the drums that he'd use to dry off. That final night, Linda took Robin's towel and massaged flour into it, folded it up carefully and put it in its usual place near Dennis' drum kit. "When Robin opened it that night," Linda laughingly recounts, "the flour went all over him. Everyone was hysterical on stage. The Japanese didn't know what was going on; they thought we were loonies. And Robin said, "What

111

are you laughing at?' And then he saw himself." According to Linda, Robin immediately blamed the opening act, thinking they were seeking revenge for an earlier prank. "While they [the Japanese group] were singing 'It Never Rains in California,' we went on stage. Dennis had one drum, somebody else had a triangle and I had a tambourine. We went onstage singing, and they thought we were nutters. Later on in their show, we dressed up like stagehands and started hammering on stage while they were singing. So Robin thought it must have been them that played a trick on the Bee Gees. He ran off stage, chasing this Japanese group all around." At that point, Alan Kendall commenced bombing and "they were going in every direction. Barry was singing 'Words,' and Dennis was behind him, firing the bombs and drumsticks. And as Barry sings, 'It's only Words' he ducks his head and a rubber arrow sails over his head into the audience, then he stands up and sings 'And words are all I have." During the blitz of the flour bombs, "Robin wouldn't go back onstage. Dick had to talk to him for at least two or three numbers before he finally talked him back onstage. By then, the flour bombs died down a bit. We were running out."

That trip was also Yvonne's first tour with the Bee Gees, and as Linda recalls, "she was very quiet. We were trying to get her to climb in a box and at the medley in the show, come out and throw confetti all over Maurice. We got Maurice to talk Yvonne into doing it. We told her we were just going to push her across the stage to the other side, and we'd tap on the box when it was time to come out. But we left her onstage, and, of course, we never tapped on the box. And she sat in there. Finally, she came out, and she was so embarrassed because she was such a shy girl." Maurice recalls that last show in Saporo. "They went mad. God knows what the audience must have thought of us."

While these tours were financially successful and sometimes a lot of fun, the Bee Gees were not being fulfilled as artists. It was more than the lack of hit records that was discouraging. They seemed to be caught up in a pattern of tour-record-tour. After a while, it seemed like they were just spinning their wheels. And then the group's latest recording, **A Kick In the Head is Worth Eight In the Pants,** was rejected by Altantic Records. It was quite a shock as Dick Ashby remembers. "After all those years, to send an album to the office and have them say 'Sorry lads, it's not good enough'." Barry: "It was some nice music, but just totally mainstream pop. They were downers, written about ourselves and things like that." The record was never released.

At a point where it looked like their days as record-makers might be ending, Robert Stigwood came up with the idea that turned around the Bee Gees' career. "I just felt that Arif Mardin was a terrific producer. I knew him because of our Atlantic connection. I asked him if he would come in and start recording them, and he did **Mr. Natural.**" That record wasn't a hit. "We simply were not devoting enough time to our albums," Maurice points out. "We recorded **Mr. Natural** while on tour. Every time we had a few days off, we'd be shooting back to New York to do a few tracks. When we finally finished, we knew we could do better work." Barry adds, "We wanted to move into an area of better tighter rhythms and become more of a band than just three brothers." According to Robin, **Mr. Natural** "was just a transition. The next album, **Main Course,** was the complete cross to most of the directions we wanted to take, which was black music, R & B."

On the **Mr. Natural** album, there are a number of fine cuts, especially the title song, "Dogs," and

"Charade," But the public wasn't listening to the group. Or maybe it was the other way around. Maybe the Bee Gees needed to listen to what was current in popular music.

5

RESURRECTION

In retrospect, the Bee Gees "transition" period seem smooth and natural, but it is important to remember that the move from a primarily ballad group to an R & B band wasn't an obvious or easy change.

On **Mr. Natural,** songs like "I Can't Let You Go" and "Down The Road," the Bee Gees were singing and playing stronger than they had in years. To Robin, the move toward R & B was long overdue. "Our roots was the R & B music, but we didn't know what direction would be best to go in. So **Main Course** was several directions, country with songs like 'Come on Over' [a big hit for Olivia Newton-John] and R & B with songs like 'Nights On Broadway' and 'Jive Talkin'.' The most positive thing that came off that album was the R & B influence. That really just paved the whole way. That's what we wanted to do, and we just thanked God that that's what people accepted that we were doing."

For the recording of **Main Course,** the Bee Gees lived at 461 Ocean Boulevard in Miami, a house made famous by Eric Clapton when he named one of his albums after the address. They also started recording at nearby Criteria Studios, the home of some of the biggest R & B hits through the years. As Linda Gibb remembers, things weren't going well. "They were in the studio putting some tracks down. Dick [Ashby] and Tom [Kennedy] and I were the onlookers, and we were looking at each other and thinking, 'This isn't what's happening now. They've got to write something more uptempo.' " Those were difficult times for the group. Robin recalls that "Ahmet [Ertegun, the head of

115

Atlantic Records] was so quick to turn off to us, to say, 'This is it?' We thought they weren't even going to give us a chance. They were burying us. Only Arif, of all the Atlantic people kept faith in us." According to Barry, it was then that Arif said, "If you're ever going to do something different, now is the time. Set your mind to that. Look at what's happening now, rather than what's happening to you. Your mind seems to be stuck in one space."

It wasn't only the people at Atlantic who weren't pleased with the songs the Bee Gees were cutting. Robert Stigwood was also concerned. "When they started the second album with Arif, I didn't like a lot of the tracks. I flew down to Miami and told them I wanted to scrap a lot of the things they'd done, and I'd like them to start again. I would swallow the costs, not to worry, but to really open their ears and find out in contemporary terms what is going on." Arif Mardin recalls that "when they moved into the 461 House in Miami, they were listening to the Top 40 and FM stations all the time. Not that they had been out of touch before, but they got into a mental attitude, a closer relation to what's happening on the Top 40 music scene."

This may begin to sound as if the Bee Gees sat down and calculatedly set out to make records that would be hits. It's more complex than that. The brothers freely admit that they did try to be contemporary but, as Robin explains, "We didn't sit down and decide to make any radical departures." The Gibbs had always shown strong personal interest in black artists like Otis Redding and Stevie Wonder. Barry feels that "people like Otis, Sam and Dave, their abilities influenced us. We wanted to have those abilities ourselves, and we trained our voices over the years so we have those abilities now. We didn't have them five or six years ago. We couldn't have done it. I think just the will to try to get back again has given us new abilities.

116

We didn't have falsetto voices 'til two or three years ago. They didn't exist. We couldn't have sung in falsetto to save our lives. Where did it come from?"

The Bee Gees singing has always been emotional, but in the pre-**Main Course** days, they tended to sound very "white." It was almost as if they were singing with some sort of mental harness that said, "We're not black. Who are we to sing like that?" What Arif Mardin helped them do was to break down all barriers in their minds and in the recording studio. "Arif Mardin is a fantastic producer," says Barry. "He brings out the best in people. Just to work with him is to try and please him. He makes you know that he knows what he's doing, without being heavy with you. It's a case of gentle persuasion." On the other side of this mutual admiration society, Arif points out that "there are certain artists where everything is sacred, but the Bee Gees aren't like that at all. They're open for suggestions. For example, I might say, "Why don't we start with the chorus, it's a stronger [melody] line?' They'd say okay. It is actually a certain creative attitude in the studio, when the pressure is on which leads to a high level of professionalism, whereby they can write beautiful melodies on the spot. A song would be formed in about five–ten minutes. One of them would drop an idea. Then, all of a sudden, the whole thing would take a one hundred and eighty degree turn.".

Once the Bee Gees felt that an R & B sound was what they'd always wanted, the music in their minds exploded onto tape. All three brothers realized that for the first time, they were creating the music they had always admired. but had shield away from doing themselves. Barry feels "We were always capable of writing that kind of music, but we were too scared. We didn't have the confidence that we could play it as good or better than others. I think the main lesson we learned from Arif was that our music had to be vibrant. It had to have magic about it. He brought the magic out of us again. We knew we couldn't go in there and make another album that wasn't going to go."

The first step in the R & B direction was a song called "Wind of Change." Barry remembers that "one of the first four songs we came up with and played to Arif was 'Wind of Change.' He took those songs to Atlantic and played them, and they didn't like them. We argued that they should wait 'til they are finished. Atlantic wasn't at all prepared to go that way because we hadn't had successful albums for about four or five years. So we went to work with Arif, and he said, 'I'm going away for a week, and I want you to write while I'm away.' During the week he was away, we wrote 'Jive Talkin,' 'Nights on Broadway,' 'Edge of the Universe.' All those songs, we wrote in one week, simply because we knew that this was it. If this album doesn't work, it's really the finish for our recording career." For any other group, writing those many quality songs in such a short period of time would be a near-impossible task, but the Bee Gees are very fast and prolific songwriters. Still, it took a structural accident to point the group in the right direction.

"We used to go over this bridge every night on the way to the studio," Linda recalls. "I used to hear this chunka-chunka-chunka just as we went over the railroad tracks. So I said to Barry, 'Do you ever listen to that rhythm when we go across the bridge at night?' He just looked at me. That night, we were going over the bridge, and I said, 'Listen.' And he said, 'Oh yeah.' It was the chunka-chunka. Barry started singing something and the brothers joined in." That impromptu moment was the birth of "Jive Talkin'," the song that started the Bee Gees on one of the most incredible comebacks in show business history.

"Until the **Main Course** album," Barry explains, "we still weren't bouncing off each other the way we

118

should have been. When we got around to **Main Course,** we finally got into a way of thinking that suited the three of us, what we wanted to do, and what we were going to do all the way. We were always split about that ever since the break-up. We could never really decide where we were going after that. And that's why all the wrong music came out, and all the wrong decisions were made. Everything was always left for somebody else to say, 'Great.' The Bee Gees never said whether they liked what they were doing. There was always somebody else saying, 'Wow.' And they were always saying 'wow' for no reason. The songs weren't successful, and we got to the point where we thought we've got to make records that we're happy with, and the other people should hear them. And that's what we've been doing since **Main Course.**"

In addition to "waking" the Bee Gees up, Arif Mardin made important musical contributions. Maurice notes that "Arif taught me areas of the bass that I never thought I could play. He'd bring up ideas that I thought 'That's very funny. I've never played that before.' All of a sudden, I found out I could play it." To the brothers, Arif was like an uncle in the control booth, helping them to produce new sounds that would reawaken the entire listening public to the existence of the Bee Gees. That wasn't an easy task.

When the Bee Gees finished **Main Course,** the group was faced with the problem of how to get people to listen to the "new" Bee Gees music. The group's management resorted to an eight year old trick. "Jive Talkin'," like "New York Mining Disaster 1941," was sent out to radio stations on records with white labels that didn't identify the artist. The radio stations and their listeners didn't know who the singers were, but they sure loved the sound. By neatly removing what had become the stigma of the Bee Gees name, the group was able to break through with their biggest hit since "How Can You Mend A Broken Heart?"

For the Bee Gees, though, the success wasn't overwhelming or immediate. Dick Ashby remembers the group's tour of America in 1975 as the absolute low point in the group's U.S. touring history. There were more empty seats on that tour than any previous Bee Gees tour. That fact wasn't as painful as it might have been because the group knew that things were going to get better very soon. "Jive Talkin' " was climbing the charts on its way to number one.

"When it became a hit," Barry recalls, "people started saying that we had stepped down to be a disco group which was sort of a putdown to disco music as well. We don't think disco is bad music. We think it's happy and has a wide appeal. It's for people to dance to. That's what it's all about." According to Barry, the fans were upset "because it was a departure from the ballad style we were most often associated with. We got dirty fan letters from all over the world saying, 'We hate the new song.' At the point when we first changed, the fans didn't want to know us. They condemned the falsettos. You find yourself constantly appeasing people who have stuck with you, and rightly so, but something's got to happen where you've got to make them like something else that you do. The fans think that because they like 'Massachusetts,' they'd like another 'Massachusetts.' But they won't accept it. Then they'll say, 'Oh, you're just doing the same thing again.' Hopefully, you've got to give your audience about seventy per cent of what they want, and about thirty per cent becomes art form. It's got to be that way. You've still got to work for the general public in a way. Acceptance by them is what it's supposed to be for. But where do you draw the line between the art and what they want? When they do want it, they all want it together. And that's when it works." As for critics' charges that the Bee Gees were just following the disco music trend, Robin notes that "when 'Jive Talkin'" came out, disco music wasn't very big, so how could we have been capitalizing on it? If anything, we contributed to today's disco music popularity by doing 'Jive Talkin'."

The Bee Gees quickly proved that "Jive Talkin'" wasn't a fluke. The follow-up single, "Nights On Broadway," was a top-ten smash in the U.S. It is also a song that includes the group's first serious falsetto work. Barry credits Arif Mardin. "Arif helped us discover ourselves in terms of falsetto voices and the funky stuff. These are variations from what we had been doing before. It was also partly a natural change. It was happening, and then along came Arif." According to Robin, " 'Nights On Broadway' was the first song to get a reaction from the so-called big guns in New York. They were sitting behind the desk, as they always do, and Arif used to go back to see his family every weekend. He would drop the snippets of tapes onto the people who were interested in listening. 'Nights On Broadway' produced the first rave; the first adrenalin flowed. Robert Stigwood rang us up also, and he said, 'This is great, write something in the middle, a slow part.' He said that would just touch it off. So we sat down and we wrote a separate middle piece, and put it in the middle."

In looking back at the shift in their musical style, Maurice remembers that " 'Jive Talkin' scared me. But we didn't have any falsettos on that. It was all normal voices. When it first came out, everyone went, 'Who's that. It's not the Bee Gees. You're joking!' But it started a new career for us again. Then, on 'Nights On Broadway,' Barry was ad-libbing the 'Blamin' it alls.' And he started screaming at them, and Arif said, 'Keep that in it's fabulous.' So we did. Once we learned that, all of a sudden, we were doing things in falsetto. Barry didn't even know he could sing like that then; neither did Robin. We just thought, 'Good grief. It isn't just screaming, it's in tune.' The first time I'd heard anybody scream in tune was McCartney on 'I'm Down.' Barry did the same things, and we all went back in the booth and said, "That sounds incredible.' So we used it, and it worked. Same thing on 'Fanny.' Songs like that. There were just so many of them that we mucked around with the falsettos."

The **Main Course** album spawned a third hit single, 'Fanny' reaching number twelve in the charts. It was certainly an incredible breakthrough for the group in the R & B vein, but there is no overlooking the diversity of the album. There is the R & B side to be sure, but there is also a good deal of "old" Bee Gees' Music. Songs like "Come on Over" and "Edge of the Universe" are as pretty as any ballads the group has done. The mixture helped make the LP the Bee Gees first platinum record ever. It is hard to realize, especially now that **Saturday Night Fever** has sold over twenty million copies, but **Main Course** was the first Bee Gees album, except for their greatest hits LP, to even sell a half a million copies in the U.S. Obviously, the Bee Gees' comeback was quite solid.

As 1976 began, the Bee Gees were headed back into the studio to record the follow-up to **Main Course** when disaster struck. In 1973, Robert Stigwood had established RSO Records and set up distribuiton of RSO through Atlantic Records. At the end of 1975, he decided to leave Atlantic and set up shop with Polydor. Because Arif Mardin was a "house" producer at Atlantic, he was told by Atlantic that he could no longer produce the Bee Gees. It was a devastating blow, Barry remembers, but "we had to go with Robert because our loyalty said so. We had to lose Arif, and we didn't want that. We just had to let it happen and not say anything. Eventually, we spoke with Arif on the phone. He said he was brokenhearted about not being able to do it with us, and that we would work again in the future if we could. 'But,' I said, 'what about the next album, Arif? Who do you think can continue where you left off?' He said, 'Listen. I've worked with you guys. You can do it. You don't need anybody else. Go away and do it, the same as you did for **Main Course.**' I didn't really believe that. We were upset, and we didn't like it because we'd just had our first successful album in years, and we didn't want to have to start looking for another guy that was compatible to us."

So it was with much apprehension that the Bee Gees went into the studio with a new producer, Richard Perry, one of the most successful record makers of the 1970's. That experience was an artistic disaster for the group, and the little work they did with Perry was discarded. Barry recalls that the group called Mardin and said, "Arif, we've seen Richard Perry and it's useless. We don't really want to work like that.' Arif said, 'You've got to do it yourself. You know what you want.' So that's what we did. It was very hard. We knew what we wanted, but we didn't know how to get it technically." As Maurice recounts, "Everybody at Atlantic was telling Arif, 'They won't do anything without you.' And Arif was saying, 'Don't worry. These guys will do it.'"

To make it as easy as possible, The Bee Gees surrounded themselves with familiar faces and places. Attempting to capture the magic of **Main Course,** the Bee Gees returned to Criteria Studios to begin work on their new album, the first one they would totally produce themselves, with a little help from a friend. Karl Richardson had engineered **Main Course,** and for the new album, he assumed the role of both engineer and co-producer. It wasn't long before one other person was added to complete the team. Karl: "We got two

123

basic tracks down before Ablhy got involved. I was having a lot of trouble just keeping my hands on the knobs and getting the sounds they wanted, and they were having a hard time communicating to the musicians what they really meant. So I saw the need for somebody else to be in the control room. Albhy was my best friend for years. He went to Berkeley School of Music. He's a school musician, and he knows the notes." With the addition of Albhy Galuten, the Bee Gees now had the production team that was to become one of the most successful in the history of recorded music. Albhy's job was to act as a musical interpreter, and that was just what the musically uneducated Gibbs needed. Barry: "Albhy's a musician. We come up with the music and hear the finished record in our minds before it's made. We convey that to Albhy who in musical terms conveys it to the band. The next step is that Albhy turns around to Karl and says, 'Get me this sound.' Karl's a brilliant technical man, almost to the point of being a nuclear physicist. And there is a science to what we do in the studio. Karl can get Albhy any sound that we want."

Karl, Albhy and the Bee Gees clicked almost immediately, Karl remembers. "When Albhy came in, everybody was glad to see him 'cause they had met him before on **Main Course.** As it turned out, some of Albhy's ideas were really good for some of the songs we were working on. So the relationship was struck up. They recognized the need for somebody else in the control room, somebody who could musically interpret what they were trying to say. It works well as a team because when they hear something, Albhy can say to the musicians, 'Let's try it like that.' The musician's paying a lot of attention to his instrument, what he's trying to do, and he's not thinking about the song, so to speak. Whereas the brothers are thinking about the song. They're not playing the instruments, so they don't know the technicalities of trying to get a particular sound out of that instrument. Myself, I'm involved in trying to capture it on tape. So Albhy is really the extra hand, he's in 'cause he can interpret what's going on."

Maurice explains that Karl and Albhy have further improved what the Bee Gees had begun to develop with Arif. "We were a little scared 'cause we were used to working with Arif. Now, I've got great respect for Albhy and Karl as well. The things that Arif brought out in us, they have perfected it to a better point and improved it more. We never used to experiment before. Now we might do the harmonies in normal voices, double them in falsetoos, all sorts of things to get a different tone. We're mad perfectionists, and Albhy and Karl are both perfectionists as well. I don't think there's anyone who can beat them yet."

The result of the combined labors, the **Children of the World** LP, was the group's second straight platinum record and spawned three more hits including the disco anthem, "You Should Be Dancing." That song was their second U.S. number one in as many years; along with "Jive Talkin'," it was the group's second top five record of their international comeback. Those were the Bee Gees' first British hits since 1972's "Run To Me." In fact, they were the first two Bee Gees singles to make the charts in England since "Run to Me." The Bee Gees new success, first a U.S. phenomenon, was now beginning to spread worldwide. This time, they were just crossing the Atlantic from a different direction.

So when the Brothers Gibb embarked on their American tour in the fall of 1976, it was an entirely new and exciting experience. Bee Gees fans now filled all the major halls, and in places like Los Angeles' Inglewood Forum, the Bee Gees were able to hang out the "Sold Out" sign. More important than the filled seats was the fact that the fans in them weren't just cheering the old hits. There were a half-dozen new hits to sing, and these were greeted with hysteria. Even non-single tunes from **Main Course** and **Children of the World** brough ecstatic cheers. Remarkably, the Bee Gees' old followers were there, too. The Bee Gees' music had successfully spanned several generations, and they were also popular with both black and white audiences, an accomplishment that is rare in rock history. Virtually no group has enjoyed such mass popularity with such a diverse audience.

The Bee Gees, meanwhile, were enjoying it all. Dick Ashby recalls how thrilled the group was to go "from playing half-houses, half of 10,000 or even less than that, to playing Madison Square Garden for the first time in their life. Or the L.A. Forum. It was like 'Dreams come true.'" Tom Kennedy calls the Forum show "my favorite because it was the best show we've ever done. We were all keyed up, 'It's got to be good tonight.' The Forum and Garden shows were a big blast. The fact that we filled those halls with no trouble at all was a boost." It is a measure of their humility that it wasn't until that tour that the Bee Gees considered themselves a solid success in America. Robin notes that "I never could really say that we'd made it in the U.S. until possibly 1976 when we did Madison Square Garden." Maurice: "We all promised each other that we'd never work Madison Square Garden unless we could pack it. But I never thought, 'Now, we've finally made it in America. 'Cause America made us. The American public themselves has made us so highly regarded.' We're glad that we've been a part of their lives."

The best part of their new success was that it didn't bring on new clashes to ego or wild spending sprees. As adults, the brothers were truly able to relish their return to prominence. And having once had and lost the "magic," the Bee Gees were determined that it wouldn't happen again. This time, they wouldn't just take from the public. This time, the Bee Gees were going to really give something back. Always concerned with the problems of children, the Bee Gees have been consistent contributors to children's charities through the years. New York City, which has provided the inspiration for so many of the group's great songs like "Nights On Broadway" and "Stayin' Alive," received the first big donation. On December 2, 1976, the Bee Gees concert at Madison Square Garden was a benefit for New York's financially troubled Police Athletic League. The brothers felt that New York had given them so much that this was small payment in return. That P.A.L. benefit was only the first step, but before the Bee Gees unveiled their master plan, they had a little bit more recording to do.

Record sales alone have made the Bee Gees one of the most popular recording groups in the world, but that wasn't the case as 1977 began. The Bee Gees were big then, but the impact of the previous two LP's was only a prelude to the main event. Both **Main Course** and **Children of the World** were recorded in Miami at Criteria. They had followed those records with the most successful tour of their career. Drive to maintain the standards of excellence of those two records, the Bee Gees weren't about to take a vacation. They had waited too long to make it again just to sit back and relax. Having twice achieved and lost mass appeal, the group wasn't about to let the opportunity slip away a third time. To deliver the knockout punch, the Bee Gees headed for France.

In 1972, Elton John's **Honky Chateau** album had made famous a new recording studio/chateau outside of Paris. When the Bee Gees were ready to record their next album, Maurice recalls, they went to France "to try out the Chateau studios we'd heard so much about.

When Elton did his album, the studio had just been built, and it was fabulous. By the time we went there, we felt like we were waiting for the Americans to come and liberate us. The place had gone downhill, and the studio itself had no atmosphere. We started recording our new album with a track called, 'If I can't Have You.' About a week after we got there and started warming up and getting used to the studio, Robert phoned us." That phone call was about to change everybody's life.

In June of 1976, New York magazine's cover pictured a disco scene. Under the magazine's logo was the headline, "Tribal Rites of the New Saturday Night" by Nik Cohn. Robert Stigwood remembers that "about six months before the story was published, Nik came to me. I'd known him from his days in England. He told me he wanted to write a movie, or write a story for a movie, so I said, 'OK. If you have an idea, come and see me again and we'll talk about it.' Six months later, I picked up New York magazine and saw this cover story and Nik's name. So I immediately read it. And I thought, 'This is a wonderful film subject.' So I called Nik up and said, 'You're crazy. You come to me about writing a story for a picture. This is it.' And I made a deal with his agent in twenty-four hours to acquire the rights." Robert Stigwood is one of the few executives in show business who operates on instinct and gut feeling, and his feeling about this Nik Cohn story was right. "When I read it, I thought it would be a perfect film, particularly with the disco craze starting to sweep the country. I felt sure that was going to build." The next step was a script and Nik did "the first draft, and then Norman Wexler came in and wrote the final script."

The casting of John Travolta and the use of the Bee Gees music were the inspired elements that made this "disco" film work. Robert Stigwood recalls how that came about. "I'd seen John T. four or five years earlier. He'd auditioned for me for 'Jesus Christ Superstar' [Stigwood's first major production] on Broadway. We didn't use him 'cause we thought he was too young to fit in with the rest of the cast. But I remembered his name, and I was intrigued a few years later to see him pop up on 'Welcome Back Kotter' as Vinnie Barbarino. I could see the potential building for him, so I offered him a firm three picture deal, pay or play, guarantee of a million dollars. That came from left field. He made a great crack at the press reception when his film deal was announced, He said, 'I auditioned for him five years ago, and I just heard back.' "

Back at the Chateau D'Herouville studios, the Bee Gees were working on their new studio album. Barry: "Robert called and said, 'Forget the new album, the live album's got to get out.' " A few days later, the phone rang again, and it was Robert Stigwood with a new request. "Robert said, 'We want four songs for this film.' We never saw any script. He said, 'It's about a bunch of guys that live in New York.' And 'Night Fever' was our suggested title for the film, but Robert didn't like it, said it was too pornographic." Robert did make one specific request, as Maurice recalls. "He'd heard a song that we sang in Bermuda ages ago. We called it, 'Saturday Night, Saturday Night' which was the original 'Stayin' Alive.' " Barry explains that Robert wanted the Bee Gees to record a version of that song "to be eight minutes long, and he wanted us to write a ballad in the middle, coming out and going into a frenzy at the end. Originally, it was for the dance scene." Robert promised that he would come to the Chateau in a few weeks with a script and more details of the story.

The Bee Gees, according to Maurice, never saw a script. "Robert has this funny way of giving us a challenge. Using his outline, we wrote all the songs in a very short time. It wasn't all that different from recording an album, yet at the same time, we did have to keep in mind the characters and the basic plot we'd been given. I'm quite proud of 'Stayin' Alive.' I think it really captures a feeling in this country."

The first song the Bee Gees wrote after Robert's phone call was "How Deep Is Your Love." Initially, the song was written for Yvonne Elliman, but Robert Stigwood insisted that the Bee Gees record it themselves. One interesting aspect of the recording of the song is that, according to Albhy Galuten, the Bee Gees never did recapture the sound and emotional feeling of the primitive demo they recorded at the Chateau. They did come close, though, and it is one of the most beautiful pop records ever crafted. It's also noteworthy that the Bee Gees didn't write the song for "Saturday Night Fever;" they weren't even aware that there was a love-scene in the movie.

When Robert Stigwood arrived at the Chateau, Maurice recalls, "Robert explained to us about this young guy, who every weekened, blows his wages at a disco in Brooklyn. He's got a really truly Catholic family, and he's got a good job, but he blows his wages every Saturday night. He has his mates with him. Then he comes back and starts the week again, and this goes on every Saturday night. But it's just this one Saturday night that's filmed. So that's all we knew except it was John Travolta playing the part. We'd done 'If I can't have You' and 'How Deep Is Your Love,' and we were thinking to ourselves, 'Wow. It's a disco film. Let's get into some good disco songs. It took about two and a half weeks to write them and put them down as demos. When Robert heard them, he said, 'You hit the nail right on the spot. That's perfect. But why are you singing 'Stayin' Alive, Stayin' Alive' when it should be 'Saturday Night, Saturday Night?' We said because there are so many bloody records out called 'Saturday Night.' It's corny; it's a terrible title." As Barry remembers, "we said 'either it's 'Stayin' Alive' or we'll keep the song.' "

Albhy Galuten was at the Chateau for the writing and recording of the demos for "Fever." "They spent a lot of time thinking of titles that would be evocative and represent the street scene of New York. That's where 'Stayin' Alive' and 'Night Fever' come from. They were both potential titles for the film, finely crafted to the meaning of the film. They were keyed in that direction." When Stigwood heard "Night Fever," his reaction was to change the name of the movie. Maurice: "When we wrote 'Night Fever,' he said, 'We'll call it Saturday Night Fever.' So we went, 'Good for you, Rob, but we still haven't seen a script. We did the five songs, all as demos, recorded them all there, but we never saw a script." Those demos were used for the actual filming.

While the movie "Saturday Night Fever" was being filmed a continent away, the Bee Gees were busy recording their songs. In looking at the movie as a whole, the most startling aspect is the perfect match of the music to the action on the screen. "Even to us," Maurice admits, "it was amazing how the lyrics all fitted. When we saw the film, we went, 'Good grief!' We didn't know. It was just one of those fortunate things that it came across that way." Fortune and a lot of hard work.

For instance, Travolta spent five months training and practicing his dancing for the movie. He rehearsed to the Bee Gees "You Should Be Dancing." When filming started, he asked that the dance scene music be "You Should Be Dancing." According to Maurice, "He didn't want to rehearse to another number, didn't want to start doing the same dance routine to a different song. It was supposed to be 'Night Fever' in that scene, but we didn't mind, and Robert didn't mind. It was an

131

old hit of ours, but he made the song come alive again for us with that dance routine."

The first time any of the Bee Gees saw the music and movie together was at the wrap party for "Grease," another Robert Stigwood production (for which Barry wrote the title song that became a number one hit in 1978 for Frankie Valli.) Because the music used was the rough demo tracks the Bee Gees had cut, they were cringeing a bit at a few flat notes. Maurice recalls that "we were sitting with John Travolta and Olivia Newton-John and John Badham (the director of 'Saturday Night Fever') watching this rough edit. The first thing, there's 'Stayin' Alive' going and John's walking in tempo with it, and the director is describing little things here and there. Robert sat there as well, describing things. I thought, 'it's not the greatest story in the world, but it's an exciting film.' The language was quite good. There's a helluva lot in it, but there was a helluva lot cut out eventually. It seemed like an X-film, and they wanted a PG, but they got an R rating because of the swearing."

At that time, nobody involved with the picture had any idea that it was a landmark in the making. Now that "Fever's" success has happened and been widely imitated, it seems obvious. In mid-1977, however, there was no indication that it was to be a blockbuster. The movie's ultimate success, Maurice feels, was the combination of "John Travolta and the music. That made the film. Everyone was dying to see John Travolta's first full-length motion picture, even though he'd done 'Boy in the Plastic Bubble' for TV. For the part he played, he was perfect. The music made the film, and he made the film. The public went to see this guy John Travolta, and the music he danced to was good. They loved the music and went and bought the album. It was a triangle of Robert Stigwood making the film to start with, having John as the lead, which was a

132

damned good choice, and us writing the music." From Miami, they went to L.A. to begin work on a motion picture that was billed as the "ultimate fantasy": "Sgt. Pepper's Lonely Hearts Club Band."

The concept of bringing the Beatles' classic 1967 album to the screen was an idea that had been a pet project of Robert Stigwood's for a number of years. Enlisting former rock critic Henry Edwards as screenwriter, Stigwood assembled an entire team of virtual newcomers to the film industry. Edwards had never written a screenplay, director Michael Schultz had never directed a musical, and the Bee Gees and Peter Frampton had never acted on the big screen before. For everyone involved, it was an exciting opportunity. It was also a chance to create a fantasy film around one of the best rock albums ever made, **Sgt. Pepper's Lonely Hearts Club Band.**

The story of the movie centers on the magical power of music, and while it doesn't appear to be about anyone or anything in particular, it is about everyone and everything in the music business.

> It was twenty years ago today
> Sgt. Pepper taught the band to play
> They've been going in and out of style
> But they're guaranteed to raise a smile

As Barry admits, "We were almost listening to our own story. It's not quite the same, not quite as glorious. But it is the story of a group that goes to the top. We were able to relate to quite a few things in the story." Maurice explains that Robert "always pictured us as being the band. At the time they were casting the movie, Peter Frampton was the hottest property [based on the phenomenal success of his **Frampton Comes Alive,** the most popular live LP ever released]. He became the grandson of Sgt. Pepper. It was the Bee Gees and

Peter; we were to make up Sgt. Pepper's Lonely Hearts Club Band. By the time we finished the film, we'd become the band."

The Bee Gees, of course, were already a band. The question in their minds was how they would get on with Peter. That answer came quickly. To Maurice, "Peter was perfect for the part of Billy Shears, and besides that, we have great mutual respect for each other cause we'd known Peter for years. It was great to do the film with him. When the casting was done, we only hoped, and he even said it to us, that none of us had changed after all the success. I thought, 'I only hope he's the same fellow I knew in England in 1972.' And when we got to the set, he was the same cat. He'd had his ups and downs; we'd had our ups and downs. It was great 'cause the four of us got on like a house on fire. We had bad moments during the film, but not between the four of us."

The entire film-making process was alien to what the Bee Gees were used to. When the Bee Gees made an album, they tended to be up all night in the recording studio. When they arrived in L.A. for four months of work on "Sgt. Pepper," they found their entire world turned upside down. Instead of going to bed at 4 A.M., they often found themselves on call to go to work at that same hour. Fortunately, Maurice recalls, their roles weren't demanding. "We developed all the characters and everything. Owen Roizman, who was the director of photography, was the man who made me comfortable. Every time he came back from the daily rushes, he was laughing at something. He'd go, 'That was a great bit you did. It's gonna be magnificent.' Orin and Michael Schultz always made us feel very comfortable, so we never felt any tension being in front of the camera. If it was a drama of some kind or a comedy that needed timing, then it would be a different story."

The recording of the music for the movie was also a significant departure for the Bee Gees. Not since their early Australian days had they recorded songs that they themselves hadn't written. Of course, if they were going to record somebody else's music, there was no group more appropriate than the Beatles. Both the Bee Gees and Frampton are big Beatles fans, so their work was much more than work; it was most definitely a labor of love. In the early days of working with Peter, Barry recalls that "we were wary of each other. He was a little worried about singing with us because we'd sung together all our lives. And he didn't know how he fitted in. So a lot of our sessions were done separately. By the _____ filming began, the nerves were gone and the Be_____ grew close together and became _____ Maurice _____ by the time we finished _____ that we were _____ other by our film name_____ Hey, _____ you doing.' We were Sgt. _____."

_____ the movie, the _____ ees strike instrumental po_____ that are _____ Peter, of course, plays le_____ guitar, but Barry _____ himself with a bass st_____ around his neck, _____ urice's usual instrument. _____ bin had on a guitar and _____ s playing rhythm, which _____ usually plays. And _____ urice was on the drums. _____ very acquainted _____ the _____ drummer. He said I keep _____. Robin knew that _____ he wouldn't be good as a drummer 'cause he'd be _____ very stiff, where I'm very loose. And I could follow _____ he beat, 'cause being a bass player, you always _____ the drums a lot. I practiced for about a good two months with a practice kit with Bernie Purdy who _____ the drums on the soundtrack. He's a bloody good drummer, and it was very difficult. When I first met him, I said, 'You're the hardest guy to mime to I've ever come across.' And he said, 'I'm glad they picked you 'cause in that last filming, you didn't miss one beat, and you hit every drum I hit when I recorded it.' I was very knocked out from his compliments. He's one of the best."

In charge of recording all the music for the movie was George Martin, the man who had produced all the Beatles albums. He found himself in the very difficult position of re-recording his own masterwork. "When it came to the real hard work of building the music tracks," Martin explains, "the Bee Gees were always on hand to help out. Not for them the superstar bit of doing their solos and leaving others to fill in. They were eager to help in any way, singing the harmonies to any piece of the film that I needed. Added to their enthusiasm and capacity for hard work was musicianship which I have rarely encountered. And their zany sense of humor gave me an uncanny feeling of déja vu on more than one occasion. They are, quite simply, super." The Bee Gees, who had first scored international fame as the "new" Beatles, teamed up with the Beatles' producer to create a record that they could all be proud of.

In November of '77, during the filming of "Sgt. Pepper," the phenomenal success of "Saturday Night Fever" began to hit America. "How Deep is Your Love" was released as a single a few weeks before the movie opened and began its rise to the top of the charts. Spurred on by that hit and the popularity of the film, the **Saturday Night Fever** soundtrack was selling quite well. Maybe it was the Christmas season, but more likely it was the "universal appeal. Every now and again," Robin notes, "a song comes along that has that. It's either in the music itself or the lyrics, but there is something about the lyric that gives it automatic universal appeal every time they hear it. It's a song you hear and never get tired of. Even though I was co-writer, I think it is one of those songs you can hear over and over again." In mid-December, it reached number one and stayed for three weeks.

136

By February of 1978, America had "the Fever." Dick Ashby: "We had no idea **Saturday Night Fever** was any big deal until album sales passed two million. When we saw the film the first time, the initial reaction, especially from some of the wives was, 'What awful language.' You know, swear words." The only cursing that could be heard in Hollywood was from the executives who hadn't thought of doing a disco film and record first.

Sensing the impact that the movie and soundtack was having, RSO Records released a batch of singles, including: the Bee Gees' "Stayin' Alive," and "Night Fever," Yvonne Elliman's version of their "If I Can't Have You" and Tavares' recording of the Gibb Brothers' composition, "More Than A Woman." The results were astounding. "Stayin' Alive" was number one the entire month of February. When it departed the top spot, it was replaced by "Night Fever," which was a number one for eight of the next twelve weeks. When it wasn't, another Gibb song invariably was number one. "If I Can't Have You" became the fourth number one from the album, more than any record has achieved in history, excluding greatest hits packages, live LP's and any albums that had hit singles before release. Meanwhile, the album **Saturday Night Fever** was number one for twenty-four consecutive weeks, the longest any double LP has ever been number one. The Bee Gees became the first recording artists to have three consecutive number one singles in eight years. Their chart domination had only one precedent, the Beatles' arrival in America in 1964. During February and March of 1978, the Bee Gees twice placed three singles in the top ten. For five weeks in March and April, they had the number one and number two records simultaneously with "Stayin' Alive" and "Night Fever." "How Deep Is Your Love" was in the top ten for seventeen weeks, from November 12, 1977 through

March 4, 1978. It was the first single in the twenty-year history of Billboard's Hot 100 to have that many consecutive weeks in the top ten. "Stayin' Alive" has sold over three million copies, only one of four records to do that in the past five years. "Night Fever" sold over two million. That record's eight weeks at number one is only one of three disks in the past ten years to top the charts for that length of time. From November 23rd of '77 through May 6th of '78, the Bee Gees had at least one single in Billboard's top three. For a simultaneous but longer twenty-eight week stretch, they always had one record or more in the top ten. **Saturday Night Fever** has sold over sixteen million two-record sets in the U.S. alone, and the worldwide sales will certainly approach twenty-five million by 1979. That means sales figures in the neighborhood of a quarter of a billion dollars for just the LP. No other album has sold even half as many copies, and it has been predicted that the sales of **Fever** will eclipse the totals of the three previous biggest sellers in history combined.

While the Bee Gees were breaking every sales record in the business, brother Andy emerged as a star on his own. Using the production team of brother Barry, Karl Richardson and Albhy Galuten, Andy has recorded two albums that are platinum, and the first three singles he released have gone to number one, the first time any artist has achieved that. Andy's first hit, "I Just Want To Be Your Everything" was written by Barry. His second, "(Love Is) Thicker Than Water" was coauthored by Barry and Andy. The third, "Shadow Dancing," was written by all four Gibb brothers. At a 1978 concert in Miami, the Bee Gees sang background vocals on "Shadow Dancing" with Andy, the first time the four of them had ever performed together. It was also the Bee Gee's only live performance since the 1976 tour.

In addition to all the success of the Gibb family,

other artists have used the Bee Gees sound to top the charts. "Emotion," a song Barry and Robin dashed out in about ten minutes, was a number one record for Samantha Sang, a singer Barry had produced in 1969 on a flop record called "Love of a Woman." "Emotion" fared a little bit better. It sold over two million copies, one of four records the Gibb-Galuten-Richardson team produced that achieved double platinum during the first half of '78. Barry, working alone as a writer, wrote the title song for Rober Stigwood's movie version of the Broadway play, "Grease." Recorded by the voice of the Four Seasons, Frankie Valli, "Grease" was a number one single during the summer of 1978.

At one point in '78, the Brothers Gibb had a hand in the top four singles in the charts and five of the top ten. Both feats were unprecedented. And the Bee Gees success wasn't in America alone. In virtually every country in the world that has records, **Saturday Night Fever** and the many singles from it have been selling in record-shattering numbers. "How Deep Is Your Love" was released before the movie in every country. It was a hit everywhere and established a pattern of hit single, movie release, soundtrack album goes platinum. One of the most satisfying successes was achieved in England. "Night Fever" became the Bee Gees' first number one record there in ten years.

The revolutionary impact of this album on the music industry has, obviously, been enormous. Besides all the chart and sales records the Bee Gees demolished, of greater importance has been the growth of the record listening and buying public. Since **Saturday Night Fever,** people who never before bought a record have become regular fans. An entire new audience has come to the record industry. It took **Fever** to open the door and show the way. The dry statistics don't even begin to explain the Bee Gees impact. The Brothers Gibb had had hit records before, but for the first time in their career, they were having a cultural effect on the world. Disco had been "legitimized." The happy and danceable music the Bee Gees produce is not confined to disco music, but there has never been a sound better suited for the floors of the world's dance halls. In 1976, the Bee Gees sang "You Should Be Dancing."

By 1978, everyone was.

6

SUPERSTAR
SONGWRITERS

While all of the success of "Saturday Night Fever" was happening, it was work as usual for the brothers. After they finished filming "Sgt. Pepper," the group returned home to Florida to begin work on their next album, **Spirits Having Flown.**

It was with a curious combination of pride, fear and intense anticipation that the brothers entered Criteria Studios. The new album had to be more than just a very good album. It had to be a worthy successor to the biggest selling record of all time. While nobody expects it to duplicate the sales figures of **Fever,** the Bee Gees are proud artists, and they will only feel that they have succeeded if they create a record that is musically better than its predecessor. "We've got so much to live up to," Barry admits. "We went into the studio with a few ideas. We wrote these songs, and know how they should sound when they're finished. At that point, we don't know how far we've jumped from **Saturday Night Fever,** or if we've jumped at all. After we got about two-thirds of the way through the album, we realized that the album is going to be a better, brighter, and more interesting record."

This wasn't the first time the Bee Gees have made a record under pressure. Maurice explains that "when we did **Children of the World,** we'd lost Arif Mardin as our producer. And I thought, 'Good grief, we have one helluva album to beat. Then **Children of the World** came out, and then we said, 'Good grief, we have one helluva album to follow here.' Then the live album came out, and after that came **Saturday Night Fever.** So we have one helluva album to beat. But we're going along exactly as we did when we did **Fever.** We're just doing it. We're doing the songs better, and naturally it's taking a longer time because we want to please the public. We want to hear it on the radio and know not one mistake is in that track. We do want to get the songs very well done. That's why we're taking a long time with it. We're mad perfectionists actually. That's our biggest problem."

"Songwriting is the key," Robin feels. "It is that ability that kept us going during the harder times, and it is the ability which created the good ones." The brothers' work as songwriters has always been the bedrock of the Bee Gees career. To Robin, the Gibbs are "songwriters and recorders of our music primarily. Performing is the last thing . . . We don't claim to have the world's greatest stage act. We don't rely on stage gadgetry. We simply go on stage and to the best of our ability, perform the music we write and have had success with." That success, Barry feels, is due to positive thinking. "Now I believe what I started to believe in four or five years ago. There was a period when we weren't having any success, and a characteristic I noticed about us at that time was we were very negative in our thinking. I think that changed the Bee Gees, and we got ourselves in a rut. The worst part about that was we refused to come out of it. We shut the door on everybody and said, 'We like what we're doing. Go away!' That did us a lot of damage. When the Bee Gees realized what negative thinking was doing to their work, they forced themselves out of it. Positive thinking means success. The only people who succeed in anything they do are the people who are positive about what they are doing."

Since their return to England in 1967 and through

142

twelve [going on thirteen] studio albums, the Bee Gees have never recorded a song that wasn't written by one of their members, a remarkable and unprecedented achievement. Their art has always been based upon their talent as composers, the ability to come up with music and lyrics that are unmistakably those of the Brothers Gibb. At the same time, they've shown a consistent growth in what their songs say and hope they say it.

How do the Bee Gees write songs? Actually, it's quite simple. That's not to demean the results; it's just that songwriting to the Gibb Brothers is usually an exercise as automatic as waking up. "What we do," Robin explains, "is just sit and strum until something happens. We don't plan songs. We'll take the idea as far as we can until we reach a point where we seem to be blocked, and then we go back again and try to work through it." Barry points out that "after we've reached our first block, we come up with a title and suddenly, that gives us another place to go. A title can always inspire a songwriter. We write a lot of titles down and give them a lot of thought. Sometimes, we're sitting there and we can't think of something, and it just comes. We just leave it to the open spaces, play along and when it's time to do that line, sometimes both of us sing the same line. And it's not just a good line, it's an amazing line. And we both look at each other and say, 'Well, Jesus, where did that come from?' "

Robin explains that the lines always appear. "It just comes. And sometimes we surprise ourselves as if somebody had said, 'Put that line there.' It's like we're picking it up from somewhere, as if somebody is trying to get hold of us and tell us that that's the line to use. We also write to rhythms. We might be sitting outside, and we must look weird tapping out a beat hitting our hands against our legs and working out a song with no instruments. People who aren't into songwriting look at us and think we're ready for the rubber room." The finished song remains in the brothers' heads, Barry says, "and we don't write it down until we've got the structure pretty well set. We get the song to the point where we can more or less hear the finished record in our heads. We can hear what we want on it, so the matter of production becomes easy. And when we go into the studio, we know what we want." To Barry, the entire process is "very automatic. It happens inside my brain. Once I've played an idea through, then I get a complete picture . . . It's like technicolor . . . of how the record should be."

More often than not these days, it's Barry's idea that is the germ for a song, but the Bee Gees' songwriting is most definitely a collaborative process between the three brothers. They will lock themselves in a small room, Barry and Maurice will sit with acoustic guitars, and they will toss ideas around and write songs. In composing the tunes for the new album, Maurice recalls the most difficult night. "We sat down in the studio for a half hour, and not one of us said a word to the other. We just sat there. And all of a sudden, Barry picked up his guitar, and I picked up mine, and we finished this song, 'Reachin' Out' that we'd been working on. After that, we got four other songs." Drummer Dennis Bryon has seen this process. "When they get a line they like, they start nattering to each other like schoolboys." When things aren't working, the Bee Gees just wait it out. The creative methods they use often have small roadblocks, but throughout their career, it is their songwriting that has carried them. They are, in fact, among the most prolific songwriting teams of the past dozen years. Ignoring their recent domination of the charts, the Bee Gees can boast of hundreds of "cover" versions of their songs by a diverse group of artists that includes Elvis, Janis Joplin, Sarah Vaughan, Glen Campbell and many others [see the appendix for a larger sampling]. The Brothers Gibb are among the most covered songwriters of our time.

Their two decades of writing together have also sharpened the telepathy among them, so that it isn't uncommon for them to each write the same line of a song at the same time. Barry points to the time "we both came up with the same line at the same time in 'Love So Right' . . . 'I thought you came forever/But you came to break my heart.' It's happened before. For instance, the day Robin and I wrote 'Massachusetts.' A song was floating through my mind, and I somehow knew that Robin was just then working on the lyrics. When he presented his work to me, I really surprised Robin by having music written especially for his lyrics, lyrics that I was only then seeing for the very first time. This happens more with Robin and me than with Maurice."

Their songwriting is the Bee Gees' way of capturing their feelings, according to Albhy Galuten. "They get a feeling. They find a line or a piece of melody that expresses this feeling, and it just flows. I've seen it numerous times. They sit down, just spontaneously, and start doing a song." Karl Richardson: "What they'll do is have the emotion of 'la la la' and they'll find a nice set of words that fits to what they're trying to say. But they're still gonna keep that emotion. To them, it's more important to have the 'la la la' space, and fit the words in, than it is to have the word and try to figure out what space goes around it." Albhy notes that "the chorus lines are almost invariably written right at the beginning of a song. That is the key to the start of the song. They know what they're trying to get across and even though a lot of the feeling is communicated by the melody, they don't stop until the words are amazing, too." As Barry explains, "we don't say, 'here's an idea, let's build around it. We don't work like that very much. We just sit and play and get a melody going, and it's sort of a throw-in from all of us. It makes our songs more singable by other people. We start by providing a good melody. The point is that you have to eliminate ego because ego is the basis for all problems within groups." Maurice: "We have a lot of respect for each other's ideas in the studio, onstage, whatever. We can look at each other and know exactly what we feel, or what the other brother is going to do next. We have a great sort of telepathy."

That telepathy extends far beyond their songwriting. Barry describes this "sensation I get if something's wrong, something's happening. It's just a ripple, and you get a feeling. I got the sensation when Robin was in the train crash." On the more positive side, Barry notes that "we'll be walking down the street together, and we'll simultaneously begin singing the same song in the same key. Anyone witnessing it thinks it must have been planned, but it just happens on its own. It's almost scary."

While the brothers usually write together, the idea stage of a song often takes place when they are apart. Molly: "Sometimes, we'll be out with friends, and all of a sudden, I will know that a part of him [Robin] is not with us, he's just gone off writing a song." Linda: "Barry can sit and watch television, carry on a conversation and write songs at the same time. There can be a roomful of people talking and he'll say. 'Oh, I've just written a song.' He says that songs are already written, and he just has to reach out and take them out of the air." Albhy: "Barry says there's a little barrel inside his head, and when he needs ideas, he reaches in the barrel and pulls something out." Karl: "Or he says, there's a movie screen in front of his face, and lots of times, it just pops up on top of the screen. Where it comes from, who knows? It's a talent. They're so good at it. There are a lot of songs that we've never even made as demos or recorded that they've written."

Albhy interjects: "The songs that get thrown away, the songs we reject, other people would tear their heart out to have. The amount of talent is unbelievable." Karl: "And it'll be just like a one time thing, where they sit down and start playing a chorus, some message that they've got to get out. I think that's why they're so dedicated and work so hard. They've got to get it out of themselves. It's not to make hit records, and it's not to make hit albums. They've just got these inside voices that tell them to do this."

As close as the entire Gibb family is, there is something that exists among the brothers that nobody else in the family can penetrate. Linda feels "that only the brothers actually know or have something among them. I've noticed even with their mom and dad, even they don't get over that line. When you're talking with them, you can only go so far with some things, especially if it's about their music." Barry sums it up. "We've been bouncing off each other and doing this for twenty years now. After all that time, we've learned a lot about writing songs. It's become instinct." Barry speaks for all three brothers when he says, "My favorite song is always the one we're working on. There are so many new directions to take our music that we refuse to stay in one place. If you try to repeat or hold on to a successful formula you die. We are always changing. I figure there are about a dozen ways to use a falsetto that have never been tried before. Believe me, I'm going to find every last one of them."

The Bee Gees latest batch of songs is what occupied almost every working (and almost every waking) moment in their lives during 1978. The Bee Gees spent over ten months creating the new album. According to them, this devotion to record making is something that they always wanted to do, but never really had the time or money to achieve the near-perfection they now seek. Robin points towards "our special pride. We work a hell of a lot on our records. We're one of the hardest working teams of people in the business. We work hard to get what we want. We have always had the talent, but we suppressed it. We'd convinced ourselves we'd gone as far as we were going to go. Who is to say that you can't shatter barriers and go past the stars? Positive thinking is electric. It makes things happen. In our lives, we feel that there is no such thing as failure. Barry and I can write a hit like 'Emotion' in an afternoon."

Molly sometimes feels that Robin's goals go past perfectionism. "He's always said that the day he really becomes one hundred per-cent content with a song, that will be the day where he starts the slide and his standards will go. As soon as he's done one song, he's striving for the next one, and it's got to be better. He's such a total perfectionist. All the years I've known him, it's always seemed to me that it has been a race with time. Which was so crazy. He was seventeen when I first knew him. Yet then, it was sort of as if he'd lived a lifetime, and time was running out. I've always felt that some part of him is suffering a great deal. Almost as if he's lived before. There's something he draws his lyrics from, draws his force from, that is very much a part of him that nobody else can get into. The things that he draws his lyrics from are so deep and so meaningful and so hurtful as well, as if there's been a great pain there."

While the Bee Gees have always been ambitious, it is only within the past year and a half that they have begun to achieve the kind of success that will make this band of brothers one of the legendary groups in pop music history. Still, they haven't even begun to ease off. Their work load is enormous; they always seem to be involved in a hit record. Yet it's much more than the ability to make hit records that makes the Bee Gees special. More than anything else, Bee Gees records have a wonderful feeling. Maurice explains that in the studio, they strive "to sing the songs the way we felt when we wrote them. Each time we do an album, that's what we're trying to get across. When we sing, we remember what we did and how we felt when we wrote it. 'Yeah. That's it. We've got it.' When the feeling hits us in the studio, that is what we are aiming for."

The creation of that feeling is a laborious, painstaking effort that combines their art with a knowledge of the craft of recordmaking that, according to Albhy "seems to be unparalleled. They're far more talented in their ability to make records and communicate these messages and saying them right than anybody I've ever worked with. The only people who I feel even come close at this point would be Stevie Wonder and sometimes Paul McCartney. I think they're miles ahead at this point. **Saturday Night Fever** saw their blossoming as producers. They've always been able to hear the difference, but now they have an active hand in being involved. They've taken the time to really get it right, really hear the difference instead of saying, 'Oh it's O.K.' We're all really musicians. We'd love to get it right, and to us it's a luxury that we can afford to spend the time, a rich man's luxury. It's what we want to do, and maybe some people out there are really hearing the difference, that every song, one right after another is great, that all the vocals are nice, that everything's in tune, and there's nothing just thrown away."

What the Bee Gees are doing is the result of years of experience and experimentation. "In the early days," Barry recalls, "we didn't know what a hit record was. Now we do. I can't put the elements into words, but we do have a knowledge about what shines about a record that makes it a hit. Where it goes up, where it goes down, where you put your colors and all of that. We work on all the details we never worked on before.

We now think, 'We've got to be excited about the back track and every instrument that's playing.' We do one instrument at a time until that one gets us off like a whole record. Then, we put all the parts together, and it's amazing." When Barry, Robin and Maurice go into the studio, they have a picture of what the song will sound like as a record. And they try to share that vision with the musicians and Karl and Albhy. As Albhy explains, "I try to tune in all the time to the writers and what the song is looking for. I just try to be a bridge between the message of the song and the musicians of the band."

It is truly a team effort that turns the pieces of music into a whole fabric. Karl and Albhy, the Bee Gees band, the brothers . . . in the studio every day as the new songs grew from a pile of rough gems into a polished collection of gold. Karl states that "we do just about anything necessary to get what we want. Also, it's never the same. A lot of albums are done where the album is the same sounds, the same musicians, the same basic arrangements, the same kind of singing. We don't really do that at all. We go for one song, and record whatever is necessary to make that song work emotionally or musically." Not everything they do works, but nothing is too unusual that it won't be tried. It is not uncommon for the production team to spend an entire evening working on the handclaps for the five second introduction of one song. No aspect of the Bee Gees' music is too insignificant not to be perfect. Barry: "As soon as something is wrong, instead of sitting around and moaning, we now go, 'Well, come on. There's another way. Let's do it. Just keep plowing.' We're all in the dark. We just keep searching for the right thing. And it comes. It always comes."

The recording of vocals for any Bee Gees album is obviously the most crucial element, as it is their vocal sound that is the trademark of their music, whether on an early ballad like "N.Y. Mining Disaster" or a more recent smash like "How Deep Is Your Love." From a technical standpoint, Karl tries "to get some clarity out of them because when you have lyrics like what they're trying to say, sometimes, they sing so high, so soulful, that it's hard to make out what they're saying. So I shoot for clarity; that's the hard thing to do." While Karl sits at the control room board twisting knobs, working on the balance, the echo, etc., Albhy sits on his left, listening to every phrase, searching for the good notes and the bad, deciding which parts of a song need more work, be it a different expression or a different combination or tonal quality from the brothers' voices. Most importantly, it is the Bee Gees themselves who make the vocals work so well. As any magician will tell you, it sounds so easy because they work so hard. Also, they are very careful not to rework their vocals to the point where they begin to lose their emotion. As Albhy explains, "we always go for the emotion first. Everything has got to have feeling. The song is based on communicating an emotion, a feeling. It's where we start from, and we can't let ourselves sterilize it. The extra time we take is not even so much to get rid of those little details that paranoid musicians worry about, but to get the emotional message across even more, to spend even more time trying to capture the one where you're really feeling it right." To make it perfect, the Bee Gees have even overdubbed a breath onto a vocal track.

Vocally, Karl points out, "they all know where their ranges lie. Robin will take the top note, Barry the melody and 'Mo' will take the bottom side. That's usually where it stays. They've been singing harmony for so many years, there's really no problem as to 'who's gonna take what.' They do try to teach each other how they'd like to see it phrased, and they all come to an agreement about 'Oh, let's curl the end of the note.'

151

And they'll do it that way, the three of them each time." The vibrato that is so much a part of the Bee Gees identity is still present in everything from their ballads to "Stayin' Alive." Albhy: "Their voices bump a lot—listen to 'Stayin' Alive,' that thing is ringing like a bell—but that's part of the intensity of it. If they sang in straight tones, it wouldn't sound nearly as nifty. The vibrato is part of the urgency."

Maurice notes that "we feel it automatically 'cause after twenty-three years of singing together, it's normal. We feel each other, how we should feel the song, how we should sing it . . . heavy or breathing, sort of breathe the harmonies, make it softer or sexier or whatever. That's one thing we learned. Another is that before, we used to get upset if one of us said, 'You're flat.' 'I'm not flat.' 'Yes you are.' And we'd have a row. We never came to fisticuffs, but verbally we used to have good times. Now, we have an actual relationship where someone can turn around and say, 'Oh no. Hang on. It's me. I was flat.' Before, no one would admit it. We would sit and say, 'Oh, that's all right. The strings will cover it,' or something like that. Now we don't. We clean every track and make sure it's damned good. When we're happy with it, then we'll start doing vocals. Naturally, we take a longer time on the vocals because they're the most important thing. People aren't going to sit back and listen for lead guitars in the background. They'll be listening to the vocals all the time."

An innovative aspect of the Bee Gees recent records, Barry details, is that "we do pyramid harmonies which we never did before. We do layer upon layer of harmonies in different parts of the record which is something new for us. They're a lot more complex then we used to do. They're still recognizable, though, probably because of the tone. We'll do everything we can. It's like sculpture or painting a picture. It didn't used to be. Being perfectionists seems to have helped us. Every time we strive for something better it seems to have worked. I find the harder you work, the bigger the rewards are. The less you put into a song, the less it gives you back. We slaved over those **Saturday Night Fever** tracks, just like we've slaved over the new album."

The bumping egos that used to cause so much discord in the group's earlier incarnation are no longer present in either their personal lives or in the creative atmosphere. Where once it was important who sang or wrote each note, now everything is the Bee Gees. As Maurice remembers, "People used to say, 'Why don't you sing lead sometimes on the records.' I say, 'To me, it doesn't matter, it's still the Bee Gees, mate!' That's what we're trying to get across. No one has any animosity on who does this or that. If it suits Barry's voice, I want Barry singing it. If it suits Robin, Barry'll say, 'Robin, you should sing this one.' Or Robin'll say, 'Barry, you should do this one.' and [Maurice jokingly interjects], 'I'll try!' But it doesn't bother me. I want our albums to be great. I don't give a damn who sings lead."

Watching the Bee Gees record vocals is a lot like watching Houdini and the Marx Brothers at the same time. The bantering between the brothers is crucial to the sleight-of-hand effect. Barry points out that "it's all part of the balance of not getting tired when you're in there and not getting bored. Like Robin will start joking, or I will. It's all part of our defenses. If we can all have a laugh, the next take is usually better. We go into it with spirit that makes it feel better. Subconsciously, we don't realize that. We joke because we're tense, and it helps us relax. The object at all times is to get the right feeling, the right pitch and the right excitement from the harmonies. The joking is part of the process. You don't just go out and do it."

"Whenever we put a mike out here," Karl says

pointing to Studio D at Criteria, "I know I'm gonna hear something funny. They come out, and before they're ready to sing, it takes a couple of minutes to get adjusted. They're not ready to have the tape turned on as soon as they walk in, so consequently, they'll make up little jokes all the while they're getting ready. Some of them are just hilarious. Like 'The Continuing Episodes of Sonny Jim.' Barry is Sonny, Robin is the interviewer and Maurice does sound effects. It's like a radio serial, 'Sonny Jim Goes to the Himalayas.' It's all very funny."

Throughout 1978, the Bee Gees followed a very simple routine. Every weekday, from three p.m. 'till midnight, they were in Criteria Studios working. Since 1976, Barry has had a serious case of studio fever. Between the Bee Gees albums and his work with brother Andy, Samantha Sang, Teri DeSario and Frankie Valli, Barry hasn't seen a lot of daylight. And he loves it. "The studio is my spaceship. I lose all sense of the outside world. I just turn into the music. It's a very satisfying sensation. I guess I have the studio personality, the patience and the perfectionism. The joy of writing a song on acoustic guitar and watching it grow, fleshing it out until it sounds as my mind told me it should, that is what keeps me in there night and day. That moment when the song is realized is my payoff." The Bee Gees really haven't taken any time "to enjoy any of what's happened. It's made us work even harder. But we haven't been able to sit down and say, 'Jesus, last year was amazing.' " Linda feels that "because they've gone through quite a bad time with the press over the years, being up and down, I think that makes them strive even harder. It's not only that; they always want to do better. They finish one album, and they always say, 'This one has to be even better.' It's just in their blood. The music is part of them."

Maurice explains that all the hard work "is for the

public and it's for us. And if we're happy with the record, we know the public will be. We want to give the people an album which has to follow an incredible album, so they're gonna sit back and go, 'Wow!' and not 'that's nice, isn't it?' I always know when it's right when I can play the album over and over again and not get fed up with it. That's when I know we're all right. It has to hit you like a brick. That's what we've got to feel when we hear the mixes. But it may hit us like hell, and hit the public like 'Oh my God, what's that?' You could be ruining it at a certain point by releasing it at the wrong time. Your timing is most important." The Bee Gees former producer, Arif Mardin, was recently quoted as saying that "somewhere along the line, Barry became completely in tune with the times. That's the phenomenon. It hasn't happened many times before, but he has totally locked into what people are hearing. And what they want to hear. This is surely his time." To Barry, those compliments apply to the whole group. "It's a matter of arriving at now. We had always done things in our life out of time. We were working nightclubs when we should have been playing to kids. We've always done things a bit strangely. Finally, we are right now doing the things for right now in a whole sphere of now."

"It's hard to know what a superstar is," Barry reflects. "We never see ourselves as that because we've been doing it for so long. We're still the same people. We've been through it all before, not superstardom, not this level, but we are able to cope with it now because of that experience. We're just trying to enjoy it, because we never enjoyed it the first time around. We were too paranoid. Now, we are enjoying it. We're having the time of our lives. We're at the right age; we're having a ball. It's not a real thing, that's the only way we can treat it."

Probably the Bee Gees' best critic through the years

has been Robert Stigwood. At all phases of their career, except for a brief falling out during the bad years, Stigwood has supported the group spiritually and financially. His role in the recordmaking has changed considerably, as he is no longer the group's producer. As Barry explains, "we are left alone to make our records. He doesn't interfere with that now. He only listens to the finished thing. One thing we've gained with Robert and a lot of other people is that nobody questions what we record. Except Robert who says, 'I like this one as a hit,' or 'I like that one as a hit.' He chooses the first three singles from the album, and we usually go with him. Or we discuss it if we don't agree with him. It's still very much of a group decision. We get together and discuss it properly. There's a good communication between us."

The level of achievement the Bee Gees have attained is a height that very few artists ever reach in their lifetime. For the Bee Gees, in the prime of what is already a long and distinguished career, success has given them the chance to create the kind of art they've always had in their heads but weren't able to put on recording tape. At times, their existence borders on the workaholic, but that's just the result of the tremendous drive and pride the brothers have. With the exception of their work, they are always with their families. Sometimes, though, that's still not enough. Linda: "Stevie [their first child] misses Barry a lot. He gets very upset. He'll sit here at night with me before he goes to bed. Barry has always taken Stevie to bed since he was a tiny baby, like Ashley. Stevie's upset that his daddy isn't here to put him to bed. He's said, 'I'll have to get a new daddy! I know. I'll get two. One for you, mommy, and one for me.' He says, 'I don't know what's happening. We just never see daddy.'"

To a certain extent, the Bee Gees are trapped in their success. They know they must create more work than can be favorably compared to **Saturday Night Fever.** Still, the recognition of the past few years has provided a high all its own that fueled their pride. It's been a real thrill to Maurice, "being recognized again for **Fever** after all these years. It's like somebody lifted up a rock and said, 'Oh, there's the Bee Gees. What's this?' Being accepted again is the biggest kick I've ever had." Along with that mass acceptance has come a seemingly endless barrage of sniping comments from the rock press, particularly Rolling Stone magazine. Maurice jokes that "if we believed everything we've read, we'd end up having nervous breakdowns, probably in harmony."

Robin, who is the most sensitive of the brothers, especially in terms of his artistic sensibilities, doesn't see anything funny in the critics' claim that the Bee Gees jumped on the disco bandwagon. Robin: "It's R & B, not disco music. Those people, the people in the rock press, are so damned ignorant and stupid. They don't seem to be writing for what people are buying. They seem to be writing for themselves all the time which is ridiculous. They seem to want to destroy everything rather than build it up. They don't offer any constructive criticism at all. What the hell does the word disco mean anyway? It means songs that you can dance to. To me, rock and roll is a slang name; rock is as much a trend as any other form of music. What is so great about rock music that these so called rock critics should boast? It's a music that a certain number of people may like, the same as any other kind of music. Why should they set themselves up against R & B? What they so often fail to see is that people are going out and buying the Bee Gees, so what they are doing is knocking the people. They talk about disco music, but how can 'How Deep Is Your Love' be a disco song? Those people have cotton in one of their ears. They only listen to what they want to listen to, and they only say what they want to say." As Barry adds, "I think the public is the only real critic you've got. But you have to get through a few critics before you get to the public. I don't want to always be criticized. We're only a group. We work right to the public. We've been to the top and back down to the bottom, where our so-called friends who were hanging around when we were up left. The people who are with us today are the ones who stuck around. They knew there was more to us than everyone was giving us credit for. I think we've convinced a few people who never thought we had it in us. I think we will surprise a lot of people with this new album."

Stigwood is not a man known for his understatement in either word or deed, but as a career advisor for the Bee Gees, he doesn't praise their work unless he means it. And when Robert Stigwood heard the new album for the very first time, he was overwhelmed. "Not only do I think it's the best album you have ever done," Robert exclaimed in July of '78 in Miami, "but I think it's the best album I've ever heard." Robert singled out two tracks in particular, "Too Much Heaven" and "Tragedy" as tunes he thought were especially power-ful. And at that time, the album was only about two-thirds finished.

During the summer of '78, the Bee Gees took two weeks off from their recording work to be part of the celebration surrounding the premiere of "Sgt. Pepper's Lonely Hearts Club Band." While the movie did not receive a great deal of critical praise, it should be remembered that the magic only works for children of all ages who listen to the music. For the most part, the press just knocked the Bee Gees and Peter Frampton and Robert Stigwood, claiming that the whole purpose of the movie was to make a lot of money by selling soundtrack albums. Rolling Stone's review by critic Charles Young was headlined, " 'Pepper' is the pits!."

The article itself harped on the film's "relentlessly stupid grasp of the obvious. You keep laughing and thinking it can't get any worse. But it does. The film has violated its own fantasy world and become dishonest on top of inane. As such, it will probably gross millions." The movie is a visual presentation of an ultimate fantasy using Beatles songs. For those who missed that message, it's their loss.

As 1979 began, "Too Much Heaven" zoomed to Number One. On January 10, the "Music for UNICEF" concert officially launched the International Year of The Child in a 90-minute extravaganza on NBC-TV. Another major TV special was in work for later in the year. In February, the long-awaited **Spirits Having Flown** was released while plans were being completed for a 50-city American concert tour beginning in June.

Dick Ashby feels that until this tour, the Bee Gees won't realize the scope of their success and impact. "That's the moment I'm waiting for," exults Ashby. "That first time when they step on stage. I don't think until then that any of us will quite realize what has happened."

It's much too soon to project beyond that tour, but all three Gibb brothers do harbor personal ambitions that they now have the means to fulfill. Both Maurice and Robin want to be involved with films. Maurice has completed work on the soundtrack music for "The Geller Effect," a picture based on the Uri Geller story. Maurice "wants to do a lot of work in front of the camera before I'd ever consider getting behind it." Maurice's comedic talents are quite amazing, and anyone who's seen his home movies knows that behind that grinning face lurks a grinning moviemaker. "Making 'Sgt. Pepper' was an exciting, educational tease. Now I know how a major film works, and I know I want more of it. Even as kids, Barry, Robin and myself used to make home movies, and I always directed. We made one, 'Million Dollar Cop,' that I'm quite fond of."

Robin's work in films will probably be more sedate than that of his slightly loonier, slightly younger brother, although it really isn't possible to put any limits on what Robin might accomplish. As Barry insists, "Robin is a brilliant human being. He's got a million thoughts going all the time. He is a really deep thinking person, but he also has an amazing sense of humor which is totally different from Maurice's. It's a harmless humor, borders on the obscene. It's very cutting, very fine." Barry points out that "Robin's intellect isn't immediately analyzable. He's constantly writing things down, just to remember them, constantly thinking. Sometimes, it drives me crazy. The point is that we all share an absolute focal point. We still know what we're doing together. We haven't drifted apart." What Barry is saying is that even if the Bee Gees have projects that separate them, they will always continue to work together.

Barry also feels that the brothers are "really behind the scenes people. We like to make things happen. Personally, I would get my enjoyment in making things happen to other people. I've had success for a long time. I would like to take the shoes of someone like Robert [Stigwood] and make someone's career happen." Barry's matinee idol looks haven't ever been overlooked by eager Hollywood producers, but Barry insists that for the time being, he has no ambitions to become a movie star. The brothers, however, are planning to make another movie together, and it will be quite different from "Sgt. Pepper." This time, the brothers will create characters that have considerable dialogue, and they will be stretching their acting talents. It's also probable that there will be a production company run by the brothers in the not too distant future. That company, possibly called Gibb Brothers, might also have its own record division.

Each of the brothers also plans to spend more and more time with their families. Both Barry and Robin have relationships with their wives that have flourished over the past dozen years. Maurice and Yvonne are the comparative newlyweds, and everyone associated with the family marvels at their marriage. Where Maurice's first trip down the aisle had literally driven him to drink, the second time around, he is an incredibly happily married man. Maurice: "I've waited forever, it seems like a lifetime, for a year like this. And mind you, it's not the money. It's because my brothers are with me to share the success. Next to my wife and son, my brothers are the most important things in my life."

As for Robin, 1978 has been more difficult personally because he's been working away from England. That means he's rarely been with his family since April of '78. Dick Ashby sympathizes with the separation that Robin's living with and notes that Molly "has built a foundation for Robin in England with the children and the house. That boy can't wait to get back there all the time." Robin: "As kids, we never lived in one place more than a few years. And as a result, we didn't have a childhood. We don't want that for our families." Still, Robin spends a lot of time in the U.S., working on Bee Gees projects and nurturing his near-obsession with the record charts. Robin is the chief monitor of the Bee Gees' records. It's a facet of his personality that doesn't seem to fit his romanticism, but Robin is a businesswise artist. With what he knows about making records, and what he knows about how to make those records hits, it wouldn't be surprising to see Robin running a record company some day.

In looking at the past, though, Robin isn't at all interested in discussing his achievements. "I'm very much a contemporary person, all three of us are. Today and tomorrow. The past is something you can never see or touch again, only remember. I get frustrated when people can quite happily live in their past success. We're not that way, never have been that way. And that's why we had to rectify things in our bad period. My whole concept of life is change. I know so much more about life . . . our knowledge of music is more vast and deeper than it was. And it makes all the songs of the past sound mild and superficial. To a lot of people, they mean a lot, so I won't say anything to change that. To what the Bee Gees were, this is an entirely different group now. We had those days, but those days are gone now." As Barry explains, "People used to say that we would never have a lasting influence on music. We really hated that. We always knew we could create music that would last and have an influence on other people." When asked what they want to be remembered for, Maurice responds by expressing the hope "that we can be remembered for contributing a lot musically, as three people who made a lot of people very happy with the music and given them lovely memories." Barry wants to "be remembered for our versatility rather than anything else, and for our vocals. Whatever we might do, I hope we are remembered for it." As for Robin, "there's no room for being just a part of yesterday. We want to be a part of now and we want to continue what we're doing right now until we drop." Robin isn't concerned with building monuments. He just wants to keep making beautiful music.

The Bee Gees' story was once filled with the heartbreak that so often goes with success. Not anymore. Now, this is a story that belongs with other fairy tales. These are artists who are still growing, but they are also artists who have been recognized as the best. With that knowledge, they have remained totally unpretentious, have grown gracefully with their success, and haven't drowned in the rewards. And through it all, they have kept a remarkable sense of perspective. In all their daily dealings, what comes through is the remarkable and deep love and respect they have for one another as human beings. Maurice: "I have a great deal of respect for what we persevered through. Besides naturally being in love with my brothers, I respect their patience and humor." The Bee Gees have no boss, and while Barry might be considered an unofficial leader, this is a relationship that is totally equal. Linda is talking about Barry when she says, "He's never just gone out for number one, and I don't think he ever would," but she might as well be talking about each of the brothers. As Linda adds, Barry "will always go out for what's best for all of them. I think in that way Barry's pretty special because he's not self-centered. Even if he's not a part of what his brothers are doing, he'd still want to get the best for them. All the brothers are just not affected by the business at all. They are pretty down to earth."

Barry is just hoping that no one will pinch him and wake him up from the dream. "When we were kids, we'd sit on each other's beds all night and plan our careers. We decided that when we got to the top, we'd have our own office. We wanted to get to a point where we wouldn't have to work ever again so we could sit back and enjoy everything we'd accomplished. A few years ago, that seemed forever out of reach. Sometimes, I think I'm living that dream now. We've never really made it before. If this is indeed the top, then it's better than what we imagined. It's a lot of fun."

Having achieved all the success they'd ever dreamed of, and quite a bit more, the Bee Gees are now working hard to give something back.

1979 was the United Nation's Year of the Child, and the Bee Gees were at the forefront of a movement that they hope will help all the needy children of the world. In 1976, as Maurice recalls, "we started it with the Police Athletic League benefit in New York, basically because New York has given us a lot of inspiration for writing." In July of 1978, the New York premiere of "Sgt. Pepper's Lonely Hearts Club Band" was a benefit for P.A.L. Whenever they've won a cash award like the Ampex Golden Reel, the Bee Gees have directed the prize money towards a children's charity. Their efforts on the behalf of children have been minor compared to the ambitious program called "Music for UNICEF."

Barry explains that "it's always been our instinct that the only real people in need in the world are children. It's vital. We've all been children and know that feeling when people don't care. Adults can always fend for themselves in one way or another. When you read articles and see things like Biafra and all the other things where only children seem to be involved and suffering, that's where you've got to send your heart." Maurice points out that the Bee Gees have chosen "UNICEF because it's handled by the U.N. and it's not just for one country. It's international."

"Our motivation is really that we all love our family," Barry says. "It is in appreciation of what we have been able to provide for them that we have tried to help deprived children who are far less fortunate. Young people have continually supported us, and Music for UNICEF and our other efforts are our way of saying 'thank you.'" The Bee Gees have taken on this enormous task, according to Robin, because "everyone sees it all on television, and no one's doing anything about it. People look at television and say, 'Oh, that's terrible' and then they turn the television off, make some more coffee and start talking about other things."

The program that the Bee Gees have set in motion is

164

a three-pronged attack that they hope will not only raise millions of dollars, but in Barry's words, "will alert the whole world to the cause of children." Maurice details how the group has donated the earnings from one song, "Too Much Heaven," and that "we're trying to get nine other artists to join us and do the same thing. Then, we'd put all the songs on an album and release that as **Music for UNICEF** and let them get all the money."

All three Bee Gees are proud parents, and they feel that having been blessed with the success that enables them to look after their children, they must help those less fortunate. Barry: "Those kids are the grown-ups of tomorrow. We'll all be wanting them to look after us. You've got to think of the future rather than the past. There are millions of children starving, and if you can do something about it, you must do it. But all people do is talk. You've got to set up some sort of concrete way of doing it. Where you can see it through and follow the money. This isn't something where you just give, and you don't know what happened to the money." Pointing to the legal entanglements of the proceeds from George Harrison's Bangladesh benefit, the Bee Gees are concerned that their and other groups' work isn't wasted. That's where the third part of their plan comes into play. With David Frost, the Bee Gees arranged to do a number of network television specials in which they would travel the world to see what effect the money has had. The Brothers Gibb will go right to the children to find out if they are indeed being helped. "Kids need lots of love," Maurice notes, "but they also need a lot of financial backing to give them love. It's great loving your own child, but it's a very different love in giving something to help another child that isn't yours."

Henry La Bouisse, the executive director of UNICEF, feels that "Music for UNICEF is a unique and continuing concept of fund-raising that will bring substantial sums for needy children. This very original idea and generous impulse by the Bee Gees opens the door for all top musical composers' personal involvement in the noble task of helping children, the substance of our future." At the press conference that announced the program, David Frost exclaimed that the Bee Gees' contribution alone could mean as much as a hundred million dollars.

To Barry, Robin and Maurice, **Music for UNICEF** is the first step towards achieving their ultimate goal of helping all the needy children in the world. That is all-important to them. The Bee Gees hope that the magic that is their music can and will make this world a better place.

With the help of some friends, the Bee Gees will see to that.

Like a bird in the wind
Like a tree in the storm
Like the breath of a child
From the moment he's born
Til the very last day
When the curtains are drawn
We are Children of the World©

APPENDIX

Below is a sampling of cover versions
of Bee Gees songs. (All of these tunes were written,
recorded and released by the Bee Gees.)

And the Sun Will Shine	Jose Feliciano
	Paul Jones
	P.J. Proby
Barker of the U.F.O.	Gerard Franklin
Big Chance	The Kids
Birdie Told Me	Peter Straker
	Dodie West
Bury Me Down By The River	P.P. Arnold
Butterfly	Marmalade
	Unit 4 + 2
Charade	Samantha Sang
Close Another Door	Jennifer
Coalman	Ronnie Burns
Come On Over	Olivia Newton-John
Craise Finton Kirk Royal	Johnny Young
Academy of the Arts	
Cucumber Castle	John Hamilton
Dearest	Laureano Brazuela
Don't Forget To Remember	Johnny Mathis
	Adina Edwards
	Skeeter Davis
	Gloria Loring
	James Last
	Lulu
	Tigers
Don't Wanna Live Inside	Sounds Spirits
Myself	
Down the Road	Demis Roussos
The Earnest of Being George	Teenmakers
Elisa	Clouds
	The Britain Singers
Every Christian Lion-Hearted	Johnny Young
Man Will Show You	
Exit Stage Right	Ronnie Burns
Fanny (Be Tender With My	Gino Cunico
Love)	
First Mistake I Ever Made	Richard Lee De Hart

First of May	Mel Carter
	Cilla Black
	Jose Feliciano
	Jacky Benson
	Frank Ifield
	Marbles
Follow the Wind	The Flanagans,
	Lionel Long
Forever	Dave Berry
Give A Hand, Take A Hand	Staple Singers
	Petula Clark
	Brenda Lee
	P.P. Arnold
Give Your Best	Glen Yarbrough
	Steve Carey
Harry Braff	Hazze Hep
	John Hamilton
Holiday	Claudine Longet
	Astrud Gilberto
	Anita Kerr Singers
Horizontal	John Hamilton
How Can You Mend A	Al Green
Broken Heart	Andy Williams
	Johnny Mathis
	Cher
	Vikki Carr
How Deep Is Your Love	Johnny Mathis and Deneice
How Many Birds	Williams
I Am the World	The Kids
I Can't See Nobody	Johnny Young
	Nina Simone
	Mitch Ryder
	Marbles
I Close My Eyes	Jone Hamilton
Idea	John Hamilton
If I Can't Have You	Yvonne Elliman
I'll Kiss Your Memory	Adina Edwards
I'll Know What To Do	Ronnie Burns
Indian Gin and Whiskey Dry	I Nuovi Angeli
In My Own Time	John Hamilton
IOIO	Engelbert Humperdinck
	Janis Joplin
I Started A Joke	Richie Havens
	Brothers Four, Nigel Olson
	James Last
	Lulu
It Doesn't Matter Much To	Clouds
Me	The Britain Singers
Its Just the Way	Morning Star

I've Gotta Get A Message To You	Percy Sledge
	Tim Rose
	Jose Feliciano
	Tigers
I Was the Child	Nicoli Di Bari
Jive Talkin'	Rufus
	Ronnie Dyson
	Cedar Walton
Jumbo	Jerry Wilton
	Chris Bruhn Orchestra
Kilburn Towers	William E. Kimber
Kitty Can	Valau Neckar
Lamplight	The Tremeloes
	G. Wilton
	Horste Wende
Let There be Love	Tim Rose
	Tom Jones
Like Nobody Else	Los Bravos
Lonely Days	Paul Mariat
	Enoch Light
The Lord	Jack Wild
	Mene Gazkon
Lost In Your Love	Lee Roberts
Love Me	Yvonne Elliman
Love So Right	Chelsea Brown
	Jerry Butler & Thelma Houston
Man For All Seasons	Oliver
Marley Purt Drive	Jose Feliciano
	Coyote
	Bonny St. Claire
	Lulu
	Hernan Kien
Massachusetts	Ed Ames
	John Rowles
	Janis Joplin
	Claude Francois
	Patty Pravo
	Los Tamara
	Dan Hill
	Val Doonican
	Vicki Leandros
Melody Fair	Lulu
	Percy Faith
	Tigers
	Paul Mariat
	Yuri Tahiro
	Richard Hewson Orchestra
	Shocking Blue

More Than A Woman	Tavares
Morning Of My Life (In the Morning)	Nina Simone
	Esther and Abi Ofarim
	Ronnie Burns
	Lulu
	Springfield Revival
My World	Rafael Ferro
	Gustav Winkler
Never Say Never Again	Tangerine Peel
	John Hamilton
New York Mining Disaster (1941)	Ashton, Gardner & Dyke
	Gerard Franklin
	Velvett Frogg
Night Fever	Carol Douglas
Nights on Broadway	Candi Staton
One Million Years	James Last
One Minute Woman	Billy Fury
	Jackie Lomax
Please Read Me	Nina Simone
	Gerry Marsden
Really and Sincerely	I Gatti Rossi
	Irene Pettri
	The Britain Singers
Red Chair Fade Away	Gerard Franklin
Road To Alaska	Lope De Toledo
Run To Me	Ray Conniff
	Sarah Vaughn
	Johnny Mathis
	Jerry Vale
	Brenda Lee
Saved By the Bell	Mike Hill
	James Last
	Hams Petter Hansen
Saw A New Morning	Vincent Morrocco
Second Hand People	Mike Furber
The Singer Sang His Song	The Nomads
	Bill Shepherd Singers
	John Hamilton
Sinking Ships	Gerard Franklin
	Neville Whitmill
	Robert Stigwood Orchestra
Sir Geoffrey Saved the World	F.R. David
	Gerard Franklin
Sound of Love	Etta James
	Paul Slade
Suddenly	Mike Batt
	John Hamilton
Spicks and Specks	The Searchers
	The Elite Boys

Starlight of Love (Take Hold of That Star)	Col Joye
The Storm	Family Dogg
Swan Song	Jill Kirkland
	Crib Jorgens
	Suzanne Doucet
Subway	Blonde on Blonde
Sweetheart	Engelbert Humperdinck
	Dean Martin
Tell Me Why	Kenny Rogers and the 1st Edition
To Love Somebody	Janis Joplin
	Eric Burdon and the Animals
	Chambers Brothers
	Gary Puckett
	Mike Berry
	Jackie de Shannon
	P.P. Arnold
	Nina Simone
	Marbles
	Tom Jones
	Roberta Flack
	Flying Burrito Brothers
	Kenji Sawadi
Terrible Way To Treat Your Baby	Ronnie Burns
	Vibrants
Turn of the Century	The Cyrkle
Top Hat	The Montanas
Tomorrow Tomorrow	Johnny Bynomo
	John Hamilton
When the Swallows Fly	Norma Leon
	I Nuovi Angeli
Where Are You	Mike Furber
Wine and Women	Johnny Hawker Orchestra
With the Sun In My Eyes	Sandie Shaw
Words	Elvis Presley
	Glen Campbell
	Rita Coolidge
	Lynn Anderson
	Barbara Mandrell
	Cilla Black
	Sandie Shaw
	David Garrick
	Engelbert Humperdinck
	Roy Orbison
	Donna Fargo
World	Glen Campbell
	David Garrick

45s; (Release Date)	Highest Chart Position Attained		
	United States	England	Germany
Spicks and Specks ('67)	nr	—	37
New York Mining Disaster ('67)	14	12	10
To Love Somebody ('67)	17	41	19
Holiday ('67)	16	nr	—
Massachusetts ('67)	11	1	1
Words ('68)	15	8	1
Jumbo/The Singer Sang His Song ('68)	28	25	5
I've Gotta Get A Message To You ('68)	2	1	3
I Started A Joke ('68)	2	—	—
First of May/Lamplight ('69)	37	nr	3
Tomorrow Tomorrow ('69)	54	5	6
Saved By the Bell (Robin) ('69)	—	23	3
Don't Forget To Remember ('69)	34	2	9
One Million Years (Robin) ('69)	—	2	14
August October (Robin) ('69)	—	—	15
If I Only Had My Mind On Something Else ('69)	91	45	nr
IOIO ('70)	94	nr	6
Railroad (Maurice) ('70)	—	49	—
I'll Kiss Your Memory (Barry) ('70)	—	—	24
Lonely Days ('70)	3	33	—
How Can You Mend A Broken Heart ('71)	1	—	nr
Don't Wanna Live Inside Myself ('71)	53	—	41
My World ('72)	16	13	—
Run To Me ('72)	16	9	—

172

	United States	England	Germany
Alive ('72)	34	—	—
Saw A New Morning ('73)	94	—	—
Wouldn't I Be Someone ('73)	—	—	—
Mr. Natural ('74)	93	nr	nr
Throw A Penny ('74)	—	—	nr
Charade ('74)	—	—	18
Jive Talkin' ('75)	1	5	16
Nights On Broadway ('75)	7	—	47
Fanny (Be Tender With My Love) ('76)	7	—	16
You Should Be Dancing ('76)	1	5	38
Love So Right ('76)	3	41	nr
Boogie Child ('77)	12	nr	—
Children of the World ('77)	nr	—	—
Edge of the Universe ('77)	26	—	21
How Deep Is Your Love ('77)	1	2	2
Stayin' Alive ('78)	1	4	2
Night Fever ('78)	1	1	
Oh! Darling (Robin) ('78)	15		
Too Much Heaven ('78)			

173

Billboard magazine chart positions used for United States 45s.

nr = not released.

— means that the record failed to chart.

1963-1966 AUSTRALIAN RECORDINGS

The eleven Australian singles, 1963-66;
The Three Kisses of Love/The Battle of the Blue and the Grey
Timber/Take Hold of that Star
Peace of Mind/Don't Say Goodbye
Claustrophobia/Could It Be
Turn Around Look at Me/Theme from Jamie McPheeters
You Wouldn't Know/Everyday I Have to Cry
Wine and Women/Follow the Wind
I Was A Lover, A Leader of Men/And the Children Laughing
I Want Home/Cherry Red
Monday's Rain/All of My Life
Spicks and Specks/I Am the World

The Australian albums;

The Bee Gees Sing and Play 14 Barry Gibb Songs (1965)
Monday's Rain (1966)
Turn Around Look At Us (1967)
The 35 songs that appeared on these LPs were released in the United States, England, Europe, Japan and South America as the Rare, Precious and Beautiful series—volume three never was issued in the U.S.

A further collection of 24 Australian-recorded songs made-up the German Inception/Nostalgia album. These songs were really demos, jams or vocals placed over pre-recorded backing tracks. None of these were intended for commercial release.

The following six songs have been released by **Andy Gibb**— none of them have been released by the Bee Gees. (Writer(s) follow parenthetically):
I Just Want To Be Your Everything (Barry Gibb)
(Love Is) Thicker Than Water (Barry & Andy Gibb)
Shadow Dancing (Barry, Robin, Maurice & Andy Gibb)
Everlasting Love (Barry Gibb)
(Our Love) Don't Throw It All Away (Barry Gibb & Blue Weaver)
Why (Barry & Andy Gibb)

In the mid-sixties the Bee Gees wrote two songs that were released as a single in Australia, with Trevor Gordon, later of the Marbles, singing lead. The songs: "House Without Windows" and "And I'll Be Happy."

A SAMPLING OF . . .
Assorted International Bee Gee #1 45s;

Spicks and Specks	Australia.
Massachusetts	Germany (3 weeks), Japan (6 weeks), England (4 weeks), Malaysia, South Africa, New Zealand, Singapore, Australia
World	Germany, Holland, Switzerland.
Words	Germany, Holland, Switzerland.
I've Gotta Get A Message To You	England.
Saved By the Bell	Denmark.
Lonely Days	United States.
How Can You Mend A Broken Heart	United States, Canada, Singapore.
My World	Malaysia, Hong Kong, Singapore.
Run To Me	Hong Kong, Singapore.
Saw A New Morning	Hong Kong.
Wouldn't I Be Someone	Hong Kong.
Jive Talkin'	United States.
You Should Be Dancing	United States.
Love So Right	Brazil.
How Deep Is Your Love	United States, Brazil, France.
Stayin' Alive	United States, Italy, Canada, Australia, Spain, Holland, Mexico, Australia.
Night Fever	United States, Canada, England.

SPECIAL AWARDS—U.S.A.

Sixteen Magazine Sixth Annual Award—The Bee Gees Most Promising Group 1967

Record Retailer And Music Industry News Number 1 Chart Award Bee Gees "Gotta Get A Message To You" Sept. 4, 1968

RIAA Gold Album "Best Of The Bee Gees" ATCO 1969

RIAA Gold Single "Lonely Days" ATCO 1971

Broadcast Music Inc. Citation Of Achievement 1971 "Lonely Days"

RIAA Gold Single "How Can You Mend A Broken Heart" ATCO 1971

Broadcast Music Inc. Citation Of Achievement 1971 "How Can You Mend A Broken Heart"

Broadcast Music Inc. Special Citation Of Achievement "How Can You Mend A Broken Heart" 1971

NARAS—Bee Gees Nominated Best Vocal Performance By A Duo Group Or Chorus Pop/Rock And Folk Field "How Can You Mend A Broken Heart" 1971

Fourteenth Annual Grammy Awards "How Can You Mend A Broken Heart" National Academy Of Recording Arts And Sciences Feb. 1, 1972.

"Run To Me" Gold Plaque From The American Society Of Composers Authors And Publishers

Record Of The Year Award 1973 "Live In A Tin Can"— Presented By Stereo Review

"Best Of The Bee Gees—Vol. I" RSO Platinum Album

RIAA Gold Single "Jive Talkin' "

Broadcast Music Inc. Citation Of Achievement 1975 "Jive Talkin' "

RIAA Gold Album MCA Records—"Come On Over"—Performed by Olivia Newton-John

RIAA Gold Album "Main Course" 1975

RSO Records Platinum Album "Main Course"

RIAA Gold Single "You Should Be Dancing"

Broadcast Music Inc. Citation of Achievement 1976 "You Should Be Dancing"

Broadcast Music Inc. Citation Of Achievement 1976 "Nights On Broadway"

RIAA Gold Single "Love So Right"

Broadcast Music Inc. Citation Of Achievement 1976 "Love So Right"

Broadcast Music Inc. Citation Of Achievement 1976 "Come On Over"

RIAA Gold Album "Children Of The World"

RIAA Platinum Album "Children Of The World" 1976

#1 Pop Singles Duo Or Group Of 1976 Billboard

Broadcast Music Inc. Citation Of Achievement 1976 "Fanny
Be Tender With My Love"
AMPEX Golden Reel Award "Children Of The World"
Gold Album "Children Of The World" Presented By The
Mayor Of N.Y.C.
City Of Los Angeles Bee Gee Day Mayor Bradley 1976
Bee Gees Best Disco Rock Crossover
RIAA Gold Album "Here At Last Bee Gees Live"
RIAA Platinum Album "Here At Last Bee Gees Live"
RIAA Gold Album "Bee Gees Gold"
RIAA Gold Single "I Just Want To Be Your Everything"—
Performed By Andy Gibb
RIAA Gold Single "How Deep Is Your Love"
NARAS—Bee Gees Best Pop Vocal Group Of 1977 "How
Deep Is Your Love"
NARAS—Bee Gees Nominated For Best Producer Of 1977
Broadcast Music Inc. Citation Of Achievement 1977 "I Just
Want To Be Your Everything"—Performed By Andy Gibb
Broadcast Music Inc. Citation Of Achievement 1977 "How
Deep Is Your Love"
Don Kirshner's Rock Awards—Public Service Award Bee
Gees 1977
Billboard Trendsetter Award Across The Board Popularity
1977
RIAA Gold Album "Saturday Night Fever"
AMPEX Gold Reel Award "Saturday Night Fever" 1978
RIAA Gold Single "Stayin' Alive"
RIAA Platinum Single "Stayin' Alive"
RIAA Gold Single "Night Fever"
RIAA Platinum Single "Night Fever"
RIAA Gold Single "If I Can't Have You"—Performed By
Yvonne Elliman
RIAA Gold Single "Love Is Thicker Than Water"—Performed
By Andy Gibb
RIAA Platinum Album "Saturday Night Fever"
Billboard Award—"Saturday Night Fever" Disco LP Of The
Year—1978
Multi-Platinum Selling Album "Saturday Night Fever"
RIAA Gold Single "Emotion"—Performed By Samantha Sang
RIAA Platinum Single "Emotion"—Performed By Samantha
Sang
RIAA Gold Single "Love Me"—Performed By Yvonne Elli-
man
Honorary Citizens Of The State Of Florida—1978
RIAA Gold Record "Grease" 1978 Barry Gibb—Performed By
Frankie Valli
RIAA Platinum Album "Grease" 1978 Barry Gibb
RIAA Gold Album "Grease" 1978 Barry Gibb

RIAA Gold Album "Shadow Dancing"—Performed By Andy Gibb

RIAA Platinum Album "Shadow Dancing"—Performed By Andy Gibb

RIAA Gold Single "Shadow Dancing"—Performed By Andy Gibb

RIAA Platinum Single "Shadow Dancing"—Performed By Andy Gibb

RSO Platinum Album "Best Of The Bee Gees"

Billboard Magazine 1978 Year-End Awards:

SATURDAY NIGHT FEVER	Album of the Year
SATURDAY NIGHT FEVER	Soundtrack of the Year
BEE GEES	Group of the Year
BARRY GIBB/ALBHY GALUTEN/KARL RICHARDSON Producers of the Year	
BEE GEES	Pop Singles Artist of the Year
BEE GEES	Pop Single Group of the Year
BEE GEES	Pop Album Artist of the Year
BEE GEES	Pop Album Group of the Year
SHADOW DANCING	Single of the Year

Cashbox Magazine 1978 Year-End Awards:

TOO MUCH HEAVEN	Highest Debut (Vocal Group) of the Year
BEE GEES	Pop Singles Group of the Year
BEE GEES	Pop Singles Adult/Contemporary Group of the Year
BEE GEES	Pop Album Group of the Year
NIGTH FEVER	Single of the Year
SATURDAY NIGHT FEVER	Album of the Year
SATURDAY NIGHT FEVER	Soundtrack of the Year
STAYIN' ALIVE	Longest Charted Pop Single of the Year

Record World Magazine 1978 Year-End Awards:

STAYIN' ALIVE	Top Record by a Group
BEE GEES	Special Achievement Award
BEE GEES/ALBHY GALUTEN/KARL RICHARDSON Producers of the Year	
BEE GEES	Songwriters of the Year
SATURDAY NIGHT FEVER	Top Album by a Group
BEE GEES	Top Male Group
SATURDAY NIGHT FEVER	Top Soundtrack
SHADOW DANCING	Top Record by a Solo Artist

INTERNATIONAL AWARDS

Composer Of The Year, Top Talent Award From Radio Adelaide 5KA, Given To Barry Gibb For "I Was A Leader, A Lover Of Men"—Australia 1965

Best Group of 1966, The National 2UE Award—Australia

Pop Stars Of The Year—Holland 1967

South Africa Gold Single "Words"

South Africa Double Gold Single "Don't Forget To Remember"—Truton 1967

New Musical Express—Best New Group—1967

Radio Luxemburg Golden Lion Award—Best Record For 1967—"Massachusetts."

Carl-Allan Award—Top Musical Group—1967—U.K.

Valentine Award—World's Brightest Hope—1968—England

South Africa Gold Single "Massachusetts"

Belgium Gold Record "Massachusetts"

German Gold Award "Massachusetts"

Holland Gold Record "Massachusetts"

Sweden Silver Record "Massachusetts"

"I've Gotta Get A Message To You" Presented By Disc. Polydor

Bravo Goldener Sieger Der Otto-Wahl 1968

Ivor Novello Awards 1968-69 "Massachusetts"

Gold Album South America "Best Of The Bee Gees"

South Africa 2X Gold Album "Best Of The Bee Gees"

Holland Gold Album "Best Of The Bee Gees"

Germany Gold Award "Best Of The Bee Gees"

Gold Album "Best Of The Bee Gees Vol. I" Polydor

Bravo Goldener Sieger Der Otto-Wahl 1969

World Star Festival Gold Album Presented To The Bee Gees On Occasion Of Sale Of The First Millionth Copy In Aid Of The World Refugees Spring 1969

John Stephen Fashion Award To Barry Gibb Best Dressed Pop Star 1969

Australian Gold Recordaward "Best Of The Bee Gees" February 1970

South Africa Gold Album "Don't Forget To Remember"

Holland Gold Record "Saved By The Bell"—Robin Gibb

Gold Single South America "How Can You Mend A Broken Heart"

Second Australian Gold Record Award "The Best Of The Bee Gees" July 1971

Bravo Goldener Sieger Der Otto-Wahl 1971

Gold Single Polydor March 1972 "Melody Fair"

Presented By The Directory Of Festival Records As A Tribute To The Sensational Selling Power Of The Bee Gees In Earning Gold Record Awards For "Best Of The Bee Gees Vol. I" Sydney July 1972 Polydor U.K.

Presented By The Directors Of Festival Records As A Tribute

To The Sensational Selling Power Of The Bee Gees—And—To Commemorate Their Australian Tour—Polydor U.K. 1972

Just Good Productions and Commercial Radio Award March 19, 1972 Hong Kong

CRIA Platinum Album Canada "Best Of The Bee Gees Vol. II"

BPI Silver Disc Album "Best Of The Bee Gees Vol. II" England

77,000 "Massachusetts" Albums—Contour Records—England 1974

CRIA Gold Album Canada "Best Of The Bee Gees" October 1974 Polydor

Outstanding Sale Of Albums "Melody" "Best Of The Bee Gees" "Mr. Natural" Polydor Hong Kong

CRIA Gold Single Canada "Nights On Broadway"

CRIA Gold Single Canada "Jive Talkin' "

CRIA Double Platinum Album Canada "Main Course"

Bee Gees Canadian Rock Champions 1975

Bee Gees Honorary Citizens Manitoba, Canada, City Of Winnipeg 1975

BPI Silver Disc Single "Love Me"—Performed by Yvonne Elliman—England 1976

Riva—"All This And World War II" 1976 WEA Gold Record

CRIA Gold Album Canada "Come On Over"—Performed By Olivia Newton-John

CRIA Platinum Album Canada "Come On Over"—Performed By Olivia Newton-John

CRIA Gold Single Canada "Love So Right"

CRIA Gold Single Canada "Nights On Broadway"

CRIA Gold Album Canada "Main Course" March 1976

CRIA Platinum Album Canada "Main Course" August 1976

CRIA Gold Album Canada "Best Of The Bee Gees" September 1976

CRIA Platinum Album Canada "Best Of The Bee Gees" 1976

CRIA Gold Album Canada "Children Of The World" November 1976

CRIA Platinum Album Canada "Children Of The World" November 1976

CRIA Gold Album "Best Of The Bee Gees Vol. II" September 1976

Ivor Novello Awards 1976-77 "You Should Be Dancing"

Australian Platinum Album "Here At Last . . . Live"

CRIA Gold Album Canada "Here At Last . . . Live"

BPI Silver Disc Album "Here At Last . . . Live" England

New Zealand 3X Platinum Album "Here At Last . . . Live"

Silver Record Award Presented To The Bee Gees In Recognition Of United Kingdom Sales In Excess Of 250,000 Copies From Casserole Music Corp./Unichappell Music Inc. For "Nights On Broadway"—Performed By Candi Staton

Germany Silver Award "Nights On Broadway"—Performed By Candi Staton

Ivor Novello Awards 1977-78 Best Pop Song "How Deep Is Your Love"

Ivor Novello Awards 1977-78 Best Film Music Or Song "How Deep Is Your Love"

Ivor Novello Awards 1977-78 Special Award To The Bee Gees

CRIA Gold Single Canada "How Deep Is Your Love"

BPI Silver Disc Single "How Deep Is Your Love" England

BPI Gold Disc Single "How Deep Is Your Love" England

South Africa Gold Single "How Deep Is Your Love"

France Gold Record "How Deep Is Your Love"

Belgium Gold Record "How Deep Is Your Love"

New Zealand Gold Record "How Deep Is Your Love"

CRIA Gold Single Canada "Stayin' Alive"

Australian Gold Record "Stayin' Alive"

BPI Silver Disc Single "Stayin' Alive" England

South Africa Gold Single "Stayin' Alive"

Belgium Gold Record "Stayin' Alive"

New Zealand Gold Record "Stayin' Alive"

CRIA Gold Single Canada "Night Fever"

BPI Silver Disc Single "Night Fever" England

BPI Gold Disc Single "Night Fever" England

Belgium Gold Record "Night Fever"

CRIA Gold Album Canada "Saturday Night Fever"

CRIA 10X Platinum Album Canada "Saturday Night Fever"

Australian 6X Platinum Album "Saturday Night Fever"

Hong Kong Platinum Album "Saturday Night Fever"

BPI Silver Disc Album "Saturday Night Fever" England

BPI Gold Disc Album "Saturday Night Fever" England

BPI 3X Platinum Album "Saturday Night Fever" England

South Africa 3X Gold Album "Saturday Night Fever"

Belgium Platinum Album "Saturday Night Fever"

Germany 4X Gold Album "Saturday Night Fever"

Holland Platinum Album "Saturday Night Fever"

New Zealand 7X Platinum Album "Saturday Night Fever"

Sweden Gold Album "Saturday Night Fever"

Denmark Silver Disc Award "Saturday Night Fever"

Gold Album Polydor Paris "Saturday Night Fever" April 1978

Italian Record Reviewers Best Movie Soundtrack 1978 "Saturday Night Fever"

Hollywood Foreign Press Association Nominated Barry Robin & Maurice Gibb And David Shire Best Original Score "Saturday Night Fever"

Germany Gold Award "20 Greatest Hits"

CRIA Gold Album Canada "Best Of The Bee Gees Vol II." Polydor March 1978

Holland Gold Album "Bee Gees All Time Greatest Hits" April 1978

Productions (and Arrangements) by BARRY:

Bury Me Down By the River/Give A Hand, Take A Hand
P.P. Arnold. 1969. Produced by Barry.

Watching the Hours Go By
Noleen Batley. 1965. Arranged by Barry.

I Can't See Nobody/Little Boy
Marbles. 1969. Produced by Barry and Robin

Love of A Woman/Don't Let It Happen Again
Samantha Sang. 1969. Produced by Barry.

Save Me, Save Me
Network. 1977. Produced by Barry, Karl Richardson & Albhy
Galuten.

Emotion/When Love Is Gone
Samantha Sang. 1977. Produced by Barry, Karl Richardson &
Albhy Galuten.

Grease
Franki Valli. 1978. Produced by Barry, Karl Richardson &
Albhy Galuten.

Ain't Nothing Gonna Keep Me From You/Sometime Kind of
Thing
Teri DeSario. 1978. Produced by Barry, Karl Richardson &
Albhy Galuten.

Barry was also involved in a number of capacities, with both
Andy Gibb LPs, FLOWING RIVERS & SHADOW DANC-
ING; production, executive production, background vocals.

Productions by Robin:

Love for Living/Love Tomorrow, Love Today
Clare Tori. 1969. Produced by Robin.

Productions by Barry, Robin & Maurice:

Treacle Brown/Four Faces West
Lori Balmer. 1969. Produced by BR&M.

Only One Woman/By the Light of the Burning Candle
Marbles. 1968. Produced by BR&M.

The Walls Fell Down/Love You
Marbles. 1969. Produced by BP&M.

Productions (and Arrangements) by Maurice:

Trying to Say Goodbye/Castles in the Air
Graham Bonnet. 1973. Produced by Maurice and Billy Lawrie.

Back to the People/Travelling Easy
Bev Harrel. 1971. Produced by Maurice.

Just Another Minute/One Wheel My Wagon
Norman Hitchcock. 1972. Produced by Maurice.

Baby Come On Home/(Have You Seen My) Angelina
Norman Hitchcock. 1972. Produced by Maurice.

Roll Over Beethoven/Come Back, Joanna
Billy Lawrie. 1969. Produced by Maurice.

Everybody Clap
Lulu. 1971. Produced by Maurice.

Bye Bye Blackbird (LP track)
Ringo Starr. 1970. Arranged by Maurice.

Tin Tin (LP)
Tin Tin. 1970. Whole LP produced by Maurice.

Astral Taxi (LP)
Tin Tin. 1972. Maurice, Executive producer.

Paid My Dues (LP) (UK title, Don't Freak Me Out)
Jimmy Stevens. 1973. Whole LP produced by Maurice.

Sing a Rude Song (Soundtrack LP)
Original cast. 1970. Produced by Maurice.

ALBUMS

Bee Gees 1st (67)
Horizontal (68)
Idea (68)
Odessa (69)
Best of Bee Gees (69)
Cucumber Castle (70)
Two Years On (70)
Trafalgar (71)
To Whom It May Concern (72)
Life In A Tin Can (73)
Best of Bee Gees, Vol. 2 (73)
Mr. Natural (74)
Main Course (75)
Children of the World (76)
Bee Gees Gold, Vol. 1 (76) (U.S. only)
Odessa (76) (U.S. only, single LP reissue)
Here At Last . . . Bee Gees . . . Live (77)
Spirits Having Flown

ALSO,
Rare, Precious and Beautiful, Volumes 1, 2 & #3 not issued in
U.S.) (recorded in Australia 63-66)

Inception/Nostalgia (Germany and Japan), Bee Gees (France),
Birth of Brilliance (Australia) . . . these three LPs contain
more material recorded in Australia in 1966

Kitty Can (South American LP that features various rare
singles, including Robin's three solo 45s, Barry's solo 45 and
Maurice solo 45, plus rare B-sides.)

Robin's Reign (69) (Robin's solo LP)

Soundtracks

Sing A Rude Song (This London play soundtrack features arrangements and production by Maurice. He also appeared in
the play.)

Bloomfield (Maurice wrote the theme song, The Loner, for
this Richard Harris film.)

Melody (This film featured Bee Gees songs, performed by
them and by Richard Hewson Orchestra. The release of this
film and LP in South America and the Far East turned into a
bonanza for the Gibbs, eg., In the Morning and Melody Fair
became hits in Japan.)

All This and World War II (This LP contained Bee Gee versions of three Beatle songs.)

Saturday Night Fever (The biggest selling LP of all time . . . featuring five Gibb songs written for the film; How Deep Is Your Love, Stayin' Alive, Night Fever, More Than A Woman and If I Can't Have You plus You Should Be Dancing and Jive Talkin'.)

Sgt. Pepper's Lonely Hearts Club Band (More Bee Gees singing Beatles. Featuring Oh! Darling by Robin, A Day In the Life by Barry and For the Benefit of Mr. Kite by Maurice.)

The following is a list of songs written by the Bee Gees but never released by them. The list of artists who recorded each one is in many cases only a sampling.

Ain't Nothing Gonna Keep Me From You	Terri DeSario
All My Christmases	The Majority
All the King's Horses	Ronnie Burns
As Fast As I Can	Barrington Davis
Baby I'm Losing You	Noleen Batley
Back To the People	Bev Harrell
Bad Girl	Dennis and the Delawares
By the Light of the Burning Candle	Marbles
Castles In the Air	Graham Bonnet
Chubby	Jenny Bradley
Cowman Milk Your Cow	Adam Faith
Crystal Bay	Steve Hodson
The Day Your Eyes Met Mine	Lou Reizner
Don't Forget Me Ida	Johnny Ashcroft
Don't Let It Happen Again	Samantha Sang
Don't Say No	Janene Watson
Emotion	Samantha Sang Johnny Mathis and Deneice Williams
Everybody Clap	Lulu
Everyone's Talking	Michele Rae
Four Faces West	Lori Balmer
Garden of My Home	Esther and Abi Ofarim
Gilbert Green	Gerry Marsden, Michel Didier, Soft Pillow
Girl Needs To Love	Sandy Summers
Gina's Theme	Eine Runde

Grease	Frankie Valli
Here I Am	Trevor Gordan
I'd Like To Leave If I May	Lonnie Lee
I Just Don't Like To Be	Bryan Davies
Alone	Peter Sinclair and the Pleasers
I Should Have Stayed In Bed	Bryan Davies
It's A Surfing World	Tony Brady
I Wanna Tell the World	Michele Rae
I Will Love You	Tony Brady
Lady	Johnny Young
Let Me Love You	Tommy Steele
Let's Stomp, Australia Way	Bryan Davies
Little Miss Rhythm and Blues	Steve (Kipner) and the Board
	Trevor Gordon
Little Boy	Marbles
Long Life	The Twilights
Lucky Me	Tony Brady
Love and Money	Bryan Davies
The Love of A Woman	Samantha Sang
The Loner	The Bloomfields
Love You	Marbles
Maypole Mews	David Garrick
Moonlight	Jerry Vale
Mrs. Gillespie's Refrigerator	The Sands
Neither Rich Nor Poor	The Richard Wright Group
Never Like This	Del Juliana
One Bad Thing	New Horizon
	The Freshmen
	Wildwood
	Ronnie Burns
One Road	Johnny Little
Only One Woman	Marbles
	Nigel Ollson
	James Last
Raining Teardrops	Barrington Davis
Ring My Bell	Glen Campbell
	Sandie Shaw
	Cilla Black
Save Me, Save Me	Network
Scared of Losing You	Reg Lindsay
Smile for Me	The Tigers
	Kenji Sawadi
So Long Boy	Janene Watson
Square Cup	Max Gregor
Surfer Boy	Noleen Batley
That's What I'll Give You	Jimmy Boyd

186

They'll Never Know	Wayne Newton
They Say	Dennis and the Delawares
Touch and Understand Love	Myrna March
Town of Tuxley Toymaker, Part 1	Billy J. Kramer
Treacle Brown	Lori Balmer
Upstairs, Downstairs	John Blanchfield
The Walls Fell Down	Marbles
	Rosetta Hightower
Warm Ride	Graham Bonnet
	Rare Earth
Watching the Hours Go By	Noleen Batley
Watch What You Say	Bryan Davies
Who's Been Writing On the Wall Again	Jenny Bradley
The Wishing Song	Noleen Batley
You	John Hamilton
	Sounds of Modification
You Do Your Loving With Me	Lynn Fletcher

ACKNOWLEDGEMENTS

Contributing Photographers:
Hugh Gibb, Ed Caraeff, Waring Abbott, Bob Sherman, Bruce Fleming, Ivan Ive, Tony F. Gale, Richard Resser, Dezo Hoffmann, David White, P. Thornton Mallaby, S.K.R. Photo International, H. Goodwin, Dave Friedman.

Thanks to the following people for their assistance in the research and writing of this book: The Gibb family, Dick Ashby, Tom Kennedy, Blue Weaver, Dennis Bryon, Karl Richardson, Albhy Galuten, Liz Koske, Baron "Beanie" Ritch, Jenny Kuik, Jan Dance (and all the people at Criteria), Robert Stigwood, Jay Levy, Eileen Rothschild, Ronnie Lippin, Brian O'Donoughue, the Robert Stigwood Organization, Paul Block, Renee Schreiber, Dwight Whikehart, Art Barry, Jeff Gold, Robbie Leff, Ricky Leaf and most of all, "Toots."

Special thanks to David Dasch and Saul Davis for their invaluable research help as Bee Gees "historians."

Thank you to the following people for their assistance: Hector Cook, Pamela Harz, Toshimi Tamura, Norbert Lippe, Helga Moslener, Claudio Conde, Richard Brookes, Masahiro Shioda, Wallace Plummer, Nicole Baikaloff, Linda De Roeck, Silvia Pomanti, Fred Kaarls and Donna Alfassa.

Also, thanks to Jeannie, Stephanie and Madeleine at Delilah.

Record Sleeves Courtesy of Saul Davis Collection

Art-Attack led by Jonas Hardy, Nolan Curtis, Ron Wong, Hogie McMurtrie, Butch Patch, and David Sparks at Ed Caraeff's Studio.